HOW TO MAKE A PENNSYLVANIA WILL

with forms

Gerald S. Gaetano
Mark Warda
Attorneys at Law

Sphinx Publishing
A Division of Sourcebooks, Inc.
Naperville, IL • Clearwater, FL

Second edition, 1999

Published by: **Sphinx® Publishing, A Division of Sourcebooks, Inc.®**

Naperville Office
P.O. Box 372
Naperville, Illinois 60566
630-961-3900
FAX: 630-961-2168

Clearwater Office
P.O. Box 25
Clearwater, Florida 33757
727-587-0999
FAX: 727-586-5088

Interior Design and Production: Shannon E. Harrington and Amy S. Hall, Sourcebooks, Inc.

This publication is designed to provide accurate and authoritative information in regard to the subject matter covered. It is sold with the understanding that the publisher is not engaged in rendering legal, accounting, or other professional service. If legal advice or other expert assistance is required, the services of a competent professional person should be sought.

From a Declaration of Principles Jointly Adopted by a Committee of the
American Bar Association and a Committee of Publishers and Associations

Library of Congress Cataloging-in-Publication Data

Gaetano, Gerald S.
    How to make a Pennsylvania will : with forms / Gerald S. Gaetano, Mark Warda. -- 2nd ed.
        p.   cm.
    Includes index.
    ISBN 1-57248-094-7
    1. Wills--Pennsylvania--Popular works. 2. Wills--Pennsylvania--Forms. I. Warda, Mark. II. Title.
KFP144.Z9G34 1999
346.74805'4--dc21   98-50485
                                                                          CIP

Printed and bound in the United States of America.
Paperback — 10 9 8 7 6 5 4 3 2 1

CONTENTS

USING SELF-HELP LAW BOOKS

Whenever you shop for a product or service, you encounter various levels of quality and price. In deciding what product or service to buy, you make a cost/value analysis on the basis of your willingness to pay and the quality you desire.

When buying a car, you decide whether you want transportation, comfort, status, or sex appeal. Accordingly, you decide among such choices as a Neon, a Lincoln, a Rolls Royce, or a Porsche. Before making a decision, you usually weigh the merits of each option against the cost.

When you get a headache, you can take a pain reliever (such as aspirin) or visit a medical specialist for a neurological examination. Given this choice, most people, of course, take a pain reliever, since it costs only pennies; whereas a medical examination costs hundreds of dollars and takes a lot of time. This is usually a logical choice because rarely is anything more than a pain reliever needed for a headache. But in some cases, a headache may indicate a brain tumor, and failing to see a specialist right away can result in complications. Should everyone with a headache go to a specialist? Of course not, but people treating their own illnesses must realize that they are betting on the basis of their cost/value analysis of the situation, they are taking the most logical option.

The same cost/value analysis must be made in deciding to do one's own legal work. Many legal situations are very straight forward, requiring a simple form and no complicated analysis. Anyone with a little intelligence and a book of instructions can handle the matter without outside help.

But there is always the chance that complications are involved that only an attorney would notice. To simplify the law into a book like this, several legal cases often must be condensed into a single sentence or paragraph. Otherwise, the book would be several hundred pages long and too complicated for most people. However, this simplification necessarily leaves out many details and nuances that would apply to special or unusual situations. Also, there are many ways to interpret most legal questions. Your case may come before a judge who disagrees with the analysis of our authors.

Therefore, in deciding to use a self-help law book and to do your own legal work, you must realize that you are making a cost/value analysis and deciding that the chance your case will not turn out to your satisfaction is outweighed by the money you will save in doing it yourself. Most people handling their own simple legal matters never have a problem, but occasionally people find that it ended up costing them more to have an attorney straighten out the situation than it would have if they had hired an attorney in the beginning. Keep this in mind while handling your case, and be sure to consult an attorney if you feel you might need further guidance.

INTRODUCTION

This book's intent is to give Pennsylvania residents a basic understanding of the laws regarding wills, joint property and other types of ownership of property as they affect their estate planning. It is designed to allow those with simple estates to set up their affairs quickly and inexpensively and to distribute their property according to their wishes.

It also includes information on appointing a guardian for minor children. This can be useful in avoiding bad feelings between relatives and in protecting the children from being raised by someone to whom you would object.

Chapters 1 through 5 explain the laws which control wills. Chapters 6 and 7 discuss living wills and anatomical gifts. Appendix A contains sample filled-in will forms. Appendix B contains blank will forms you can cut out or photocopy.

You can prepare your own will quickly and easily by using the forms out of the book, or by photocopying them, or you can retype the material on blank paper. The small amount of time it takes to do this can give you and your heirs the peace of mind of knowing that your estate will be distributed according to your wishes.

A surprising number of people have had their estates pass to the wrong parties because of a simple lack of knowledge. Before using any of the forms in appendix A, you should read and understand the previous chapters in this book.

In each example given you might ask, "What if my spouse dies first?" or "What if the children are grown?" and then the answer might be different. You are advised to seek the advice of an attorney if your situation is at all complicated. In many communities, wills are available for very reasonable prices. No book of this type can cover every contingency in every case, but a knowledge of the basics will help you make the right decisions regarding your property.

Basic Rules You Should Know

1

Will Terminology

Decedent is a term used to refer to a person who has passed away. A person who dies leaving a will dies *testate* and is the *testator*. A person who dies without a will dies *intestate*. As you will see throughout this book, the law treats the estate of a person dying testate differently than the estate of a person dying intestate.

What Is a Will?

A will is a document you can use to control who gets your property, who will be guardian of your children, and who will manage your estate.

How a Will Is Used

Some people think a will avoids probate. It does not. A will is the document used in probate to determine who receives your property. It also appoints guardians and personal representatives.

AVOIDING
PROBATE

If you wish to avoid probate, you need to use methods other than a will, such as joint ownership, life insurance, or living trusts. We will discuss the first two of these later in this chapter. For information on living trusts, see *Living Trusts and Simple Ways to Avoid Probate* by Karen Ann Rolcik, published by Sourcebooks, Inc.

You may not need a will if you can successfully avoid probate with all of your property. However, everyone should have a will in case some property is forgotten or received just prior to death, and for some reason, does not avoid probate.

JOINT TENANCY AVOIDS PROBATE

Property that is owned in *joint tenancy* with right of survivorship does not pass under a will. If a will gives property to one person but it is already in a joint account with another person, the will is usually ignored and the joint owner of the account gets the property. This is because the property in the account avoids probate and passes directly to the joint owner. A will only controls property that goes through probate. There are exceptions to this rule. If money is put into a joint account only for convenience, it might pass under the will; but if the joint owner does not give it up, it could take an expensive court battle to get it back.

Putting property into joint tenancy does not give absolute rights to it. If the estate owes estate taxes, the recipient of joint tenancy property may have to contribute to the tax payment. Also, Pennsylvania give spouses a right to property that is in joint accounts with other people. This is explained later in this chapter.

EXAMPLE

☞ Ted and his wife want all of their property to go to the survivor of them. They put their house, cars, bank accounts and brokerage accounts in joint ownership. When Ted dies his wife only has to show his death certificate to get all the property transferred to her name. No probate or will is necessary.

☞ After Ted's death his wife, Michelle puts all of the property and accounts into joint ownership with her son, Mark. Upon her death Mark needs only to present her death certificate to have everything transferred into his name. No probate or will is necessary.

JOINT TENANCY OVERRULES YOUR WILL

If all property is in joint ownership or if all property is distributed through a will, things are simple. But when some property passes by each method, a person's plans may not go right.

EXAMPLES

☞ Bill's will leaves all his property to his sister, Mary. Bill dies owning a house jointly with his wife, Joan, and a bank account jointly with his son, Don. Upon Bill's death Joan gets the house, Don gets the bank account and his sister, Mary, gets nothing.

☞ Betty's will leaves half her assets to Ann and half her assets to George. Betty dies owning $1,000,000 in stock jointly with George and a car in her name alone. Ann gets only a half interest in the car. George gets all the stock and a half interest in the car.

☞ John's will leaves all his property equally to his five children. Before going in the hospital he puts his oldest son, Harry, as a joint owner of his accounts. John dies and Harry gets all of his assets. The rest of the children get nothing.

In each of these cases the property went to a person it probably shouldn't have because the decedent didn't realize that joint ownership overruled their will. In some families this might not be a problem. Harry might divide the property equally (and possibly pay a gift tax.) But in many cases Harry would just keep everything and the family would never talk to him again, or take him to court.

JOINT TENANCY CAN BE RISKY

In many cases joint property can be an ideal way to own property and avoid probate. However it does have risks. If you put your real estate in joint ownership with someone, you cannot sell it or mortgage it without that person's signature. If you put your bank account in joint ownership with someone they can take out all of your money.

EXAMPLES

☞ Alice put her house in joint ownership with her son. She later married Ed and moved in with him. She wanted to sell her house and to invest the money for income. Her son refused to sign the deed because he wanted to keep the home in the family. She was in court for ten months getting her house back and the judge almost refused to do it.

☞ Alex put his bank accounts into joint ownership with his daughter Mary to avoid probate. Mary fell in love with Doug who was in trouble with the law. Doug talked Mary into "borrowing" $30,000 from the account for a "business deal" that went sour. Later she "borrowed" $25,000 more to pay Doug's bail bond. Alex didn't find out until it was too late that his money was gone.

"TENANCY IN COMMON" DOES NOT AVOID PROBATE

In Pennsylvania, there are three basic ways to own property: joint tenancy with right of survivorship; tenancy in common; and, the estate by the entireties. Joint tenancy with right of survivorship means when one owner of the property dies the survivor or survivors automatically get the decedent's share. *Tenancy in common* means—when one owner dies, that owner's share of the property goes to his or her heirs or beneficiaries under the will. An estate by the entireties is like joint tenancy with right of survivorship, but it only applies to a married couple.

EXAMPLES

☛ Tom and Marcia bought a house and lived together for twenty years. However, the deed did not specify joint tenancy. When Tom died his brother inherited his half of the house and it had to be sold because Marcia could not afford to buy it from him.

☛ Lindsay and her husband Rocky bought a house. When Rocky suddenly died, Lindsay obtained full ownership of the house by filing a death certificate at the courthouse. That was because the deed to the house stated that they were husband and wife so presumably ownership was tenancy by the entireties.

A Spouse Can Overrule a Will

Under Pennsylvania law, a surviving spouse is entitled to one-third of certain property of the decedent no matter what the will states. This is sometimes called the *forced share* or *elective share*. However, in Pennsylvania a decedent must have been a married person domiciled in the state in order for the surviving spouse to take a one-third share. Generally, a person's *domicile* is the place where he is physically present with the intent to live and remain for the indefinite future. The place of a person's primary home or where he spends most of his time is likely to be considered his domicile. Some examples of elective share property are listed below.

Under Pennsylvania law, no matter what the will states, a surviving spouse may elect to take a one-third share of:

☛ Any property that would pass from a decedent under a will or property that would pass from a decedent who died without a will.

☛ A trust set up by the decedent which he had the power to revoke during his lifetime.

☛ A joint bank account with another person set up by the decedent during the marriage. A surviving spouse may elect to take one-third of the decedent's interest in the account, for example, one-third of one-half of the account.

☞ A joint annuity purchased by the decedent during the marriage that was paying annuity payments to the decedent at the time of his death.

☞ Any property transferred by the decedent in contemplation of death. Since such transfers are usually close in time to the date of death, the transfer must occur during the marriage and within one year of death. The surviving spouse is entitled to one-third of the amount of the property that exceeds $3,000.

The above-list contains only examples and is by no means exclusive. There may be other property a surviving spouse may be entitled to under the elective share. If you are not sure whether specific property is subject to the elective share, you may want to consult a lawyer.

EXAMPLES   ☞ John's will leaves all of his property to his children of a prior marriage and nothing to his wife who is already wealthy. The wife still gets one-third of *elective share* property and the children divide the remaining two-thirds.

☞ Mary puts half of her property in a joint account with her brother and in her will she leaves all of her other property to her sister who is ill. When she dies, if her husband takes an elective share, he would get one-third of Mary's one-half interest in the account. Of course, this also entitles Mary's husband to one-third of the rest of Mary's *elective share* property.

OVERRULING A SPOUSE'S SHARE

One way to avoid a spouse's forced share is to have a life insurance policy naming someone other than the surviving spouse as beneficiary of the proceeds of insurance. Another way is to sign an agreement with your spouse either before or after the marriage.

EXAMPLE   ☞ Dan has a life insurance policy in his name with his daughter as sole beneficiary. He owns his bank accounts jointly with his brother. If he dies, his wife may elect to take a one-third share of his joint bank account interests (one-third of 50%). However, this does not entitle Dan's wife to a one-third share of the life insurance proceeds he left to his daughter.

I/T/F BANK ACCOUNTS

One way of keeping bank accounts out of your estate and still retaining control is to title them *in trust for* or I/T/F and name a beneficiary. No one except you can get the money until your death, and on death it immediately goes directly to the person you name without a will or probate proceeding. These are called *Totten Trusts* after the man who had to go to court to prove they were legal.

EXAMPLE
    ☞   Rich opened a bank account in the name of "Rich, I/T/F Mary." If Rich dies, the money automatically goes to Mary. Prior to his death, Mary has no control over or knowledge of the account and Rich can take Mary's name off the account at any time.

REGISTRATION OF SECURITIES IN TRANSFER ON DEATH OR PAY ON DEATH (POD) FORM

At the end if 1996, the Pennsylvania legislature passed a law allowing the registration of securities and the designation of a beneficiary who would take ownership of the securities upon the death of the owner. Registration in "beneficiary form" as it is called, is indicated by the words "transfer on death" or "TOD", or by the words "pay on death" or "POD" after the name of the registered owner and before the name of the beneficiary. On the death of the owner, ownership of the security is transferred to the beneficiary.

The transfer of the securities on death is still subject to inheritance unless, of course, the transfer is exempt for some other reason, such as transfer from one spouse upon the death of the other. Check with your broker or financial institution for the proper forms to register, as well as any terms and conditions. If they do not offer such registration, it would be worth changing to one who does.

No Homestead in Pennsylvania

A homestead for estate purposes is property that is the permanent residence of a legal resident of a state who has a spouse or minor children and owns the property in his or her name alone. Some states have special rules as to who can inherit a homestead. However, Pennsylvania presently has no provision concerning homesteads.

Family Exemption

In Pennsylvania, the surviving spouse of any person dying domiciled in the state is entitled to an *exemption* to the value of $3,500. The surviving spouse can claim the exemption and be paid in real property (real estate), personal property, or both. However, specific property left by a person cannot be used to satisfy the exemption unless all other assets are unavailable.

If, for some reason, a surviving spouse does not claim the exemption, the children who are members of the same household as the decedent may claim it. If there are no such children, then the parent or parents of the decedent who are members of the same household may claim the exemption.

EXAMPLE ☞ Donna dies with a will giving half her property to her husband and half to her grown son from a previous marriage. Donna's property consists of $10,000 in cash. Donna's husband may be able to get $3,500 as a family exemption. Then he and the son would split the remaining $6,500. (The son may receive even less if the husband also claimed a *spouse's share* as described on page 9.)

To reduce the possibility of having property claimed under the family exemption, it may be *specifically* given to someone in a will. If certain items are specifically given to certain persons, those items will be considered to satisfy the family exemption only after all nonspecific property is unavailable. For example, if you keep cash in a joint or I/T/F bank account, it would go to the joint owner or beneficiary and not be used as the family exemption.

GETTING MARRIED AUTOMATICALLY CHANGES YOUR WILL

If you get married after making your will and do not rewrite it after the wedding, your spouse gets a share of your estate as if you had no will unless: you have a pre-nuptial agreement; your will gives your surviving spouse a greater share; or, it appears your will was made in contemplation of marriage to your surviving spouse.

EXAMPLE ☞ John made out his will leaving everything to his physically challenged brother. When he married Joan, an heiress with plenty of money, he didn't change his will because he still wanted his brother to get his estate. However when he died, Joan got one-third of the estate John wanted his brother to have.

HAVING CHILDREN AUTOMATICALLY CHANGES YOUR WILL

If you have a child after making your will and do not rewrite it, the child gets a share of your estate as if you were unmarried and without a will. Your child receives his or her share out of your property that does not pass to your surviving spouse.

EXAMPLE ☞ Dave makes a will leaving half his estate to his sister. His three children will share the other half. He later has another child and doesn't revise his will. Upon his death, his fourth child will get one quarter of his estate, his sister will get three-eighths, and the other three children will each receive one-eighth of the estate.

HOW YOUR DEBTS ARE PAID

One of the duties of the person administering an estate is to pay the debts of the decedent. Before an estate is distributed the legitimate debts must be ascertained and paid.

An exception is *secured debts*, these are debts that are protected by a lien against property, like a home loan or a car loan. In the case of a secured debt, the loan does not have to be paid before the property is distributed.

EXAMPLE ☛ John owns a $100,000 house with a $80,000 mortgage and he has $100,000 in the bank. If he leaves the house to his brother and the bank account to his sister then his brother would get the home but would owe the 80,000 mortgage.

What if your debts are more than your property? Today, unlike hundreds of years ago, people cannot inherit other peoples' debts. A person's property is used to pay their probate and funeral expenses first and if there is not enough to pay their debts then the creditors are out of luck. However, if a person leaves property to people and does not have enough assets to pay his or her debts then the property will be sold to pay the debts.

EXAMPLE ☛ Jeb's will leaves all of his property to his three children. At the time of his death, Jeb has $30,000 in medical bills, $11,000 in credit card debt, and his only assets are his car and $5,000 in stock. The car and stock would be sold and the funeral bill and probate fees paid out of the proceeds. If any money was left it would go to the creditors and nothing would be left for the children. The children would not have to pay the medical bills or credit card debt.

ESTATE AND INHERITANCE TAXES

Pennsylvania imposes an *inheritance* tax on transfers of property made by a will or someone dying without a will. The inheritance tax rate is 6% on the transfer of property to grandparents, parents, lineal descendants, or the parents of a child; the transferrance to any other person is a 15% rate. Property transferred to a husband or wife is not taxed.

Certain exemptions apply, such as on the transfer of proceeds of a life insurance policy on the life of the decendent or estates valued at $200,000 or less.

In most cases, Pennsylvania does not have an *estate* tax. The only time estate taxes would be paid to the state of Pennsylvania would be if the estate was subject to federal estate taxes and a credit was allowed for state taxes. Then these taxes would be paid to the state and credited against the federal tax due.

Since estate and inheritance tax matters can become very complicated and if you are concerned about maximizing tax benenfits, you should consult an attorney who specializes in this area.

There is a federal estate tax for estates above a certain amount. Estates below that amount are allowed a *unified credit* which exempts them from tax. The unified credit applies to the estate a person can leave at death and to gifts during his or her lifetime. In 1999, the amount exempted by the unified credit is $650,000 but it will rise to $1,000,000 by the year 2006. The amount will change according to the schedule on the following page. There are proposals before Congress to raise the limits sooner, but none had passed by the time of publication.

Year	Amount
1999	$650,000
2000-2001	$675,000
2002-2003	$700,000
2004	$850,000
2005	$950,000
2006	$1,000,000

ANNUAL EXCLUSION

When a person makes a gift, that gift is subtracted from the amount entitled to the unified credit available to his or her estate at death. However, a person is allowed to make gifts of up to $10,000 per person per year without having these subtracted from the unified credit. This means a married couple can make gifts of up to $20,000 per person. The Taxpayer Relief Act of 1997 provided that this exclusion amount will be adjusted for inflation.

Do You Need a Pennsylvania Will? 2

What a Will Can Do

A will allows you to decide who gets your property after your death. You can give specific personal items to certain persons and decide which of your friends or relatives deserve a greater share of your estate. You can leave gifts to schools and charities.

A will allows you to decide who will be the personal representative of your estate. A *personal representative* is the person who gathers all your assets and distributes them to the beneficiaries. Personal representatives are also called *executors*. With a will you can provide that your personal representative does not have to post a surety bond with the court in order to serve and this can save your estate some money.

A will allows you to choose a guardian for your minor children. This way you can avoid fights among relatives and make sure the best person raises your children. You may also appoint separate guardians over your children and over their money. For example you may appoint your sister as guardian over your children and your father as guardian over their money. That way a second person could keep an eye on how their money was being spent.

You can set up a trust to provide that your property is not distributed immediately. Many people feel that their children would not be ready to handle large sums of money at the age of eighteen. A will can direct that the money is held until the children are twenty-one or twenty-five or older.

WHAT IF YOU HAVE NO WILL?

If you do not have a will, Pennsylvania law says that your property shall be distributed as follows:

☛ If you leave a spouse and no children or parents, your spouse gets your entire estate.

☛ If you leave a spouse and one or more parents but no children, then your spouse gets the first $30,000 and half of the balance. Your surviving parents get equal shares of the remainder.

☛ If you leave a spouse and children who are all children of your spouse, then your spouse gets the first $30,000 and half of the balance. The children get equal shares of the remainder.

☛ If you leave a spouse and at least one child who is not your spouse's child then your spouse gets half of your estate and all of your children get equal shares of the other half.

☛ If you leave no spouse, all of your children get equal shares of your estate.

☛ If you leave no spouse and no children then your estate would go to the highest persons on the following list who are living.
  • Your parents
  • Your brothers and sisters, or their children
  • Your grandparents
  • Your uncles and aunts or their descendants
  • The Commonwealth of Pennsylvania

Is Your Out-of-State Will Valid in Pennsylvania?

A will that is valid in another state would probably be valid to pass property in Pennsylvania. However, an out-of-state will should be *self-proved* by an acknowledgment (statement or recognition) of the testator and affidavits of witnesses made before a notary of the state where the will is executed. However, if the will is contested or it is signed by the testator's mark or by another person for him, witnesses from the former state may be required to appear and testify. Because of the expense and delay this may involve, it is prudent to execute a new will after moving to Pennsylvania.

If executing a new will is not your desire, it is wise to have your will *self-proved* so that the witnesses never have to be called in to take an oath. With special self-proving language in your will the witnesses take the oath at the time of signing and never have to be seen again.

Who Can Make a Pennsylvania Will?

Any person who is eighteen or more years of age and of sound mind.

What a Will Cannot Do

A will cannot direct that anything illegal be done and it cannot put unreasonable conditions on a gift. A provision that your daughter gets all of your property if she divorces her husband would be ignored by the court. She would get the property with no conditions attached. If you wish to include conditions in your will, consult an attorney.

A will cannot leave money or property to an animal because animals cannot legally own property. If you wish to care for an animal after your death you should leave it in trust or to a friend whom you know will care for the animal.

WHO CAN USE A SIMPLE WILL?

The wills in this book will pass your property whether your estate is $1,000 or $100,000,000. However, if your estate is over $650,000 (this amount will rise to $1,000,000 by the year 2006) then you might be able to avoid estate taxes by using a trust or other tax-saving device. The larger your estate the more you can save on estate taxes by doing more complicated planning. If you have a large estate and are concerned about estate taxes you should consult an estate planning attorney or a book on estate planning.

WHO SHOULD NOT USE A SIMPLE WILL?

WILL CONTEST

If you expect that there may be a fight over your estate or that someone might contest your will's validity, you should consult a lawyer. If you leave less than the statutory share of your estate to your spouse or if you leave one or more of your children out of your will, it is likely that someone will contest your will.

COMPLICATED ESTATES

If you are the beneficiary of a trust or have any complications in your legal relationships, you may need special provisions in your will.

BLIND OR UNABLE TO WRITE

A person who is blind or who can sign only with an "X" should also consult a lawyer about the proper way to make and execute a will.

ESTATES OVER $650,000

If you expect to have over $650,000 (this amount will rise to $1,000,000 by the year 2006) at the time of your death, you may want to consult with a CPA or tax attorney regarding tax consequences.

CONDITIONS

If you wish to put some sort of conditions or restrictions on the property you leave you should consult a lawyer. For example, if you want to leave money to your brother only if he quits smoking, or to a hospital only if they name a wing in your honor, you should consult an attorney to be sure that your conditions are valid in your state.

How to Make a Simple Will 3

Identifying Parties in Your Will

PEOPLE

When making your will, it is important to correctly identify the persons you name in your will. In some families, names differ only by middle initial or by Jr. or Sr. Be sure to check the names before you make your will. You can also add your relationship to the party, and their location such as "my cousin, Billy DeLyon of Philadelphia, Pennsylvania."

ORGANIZATIONS

The same applies to organizations and charities. For example, there are more than one group using the words "cancer society" or "heart association" in their names. Be sure to get the correct name of the group you intend to leave your gift, and be specific in naming it.

Personal Property

Because people acquire and dispose of personal property so often, it is not advisable to list a lot of small items in your will. Otherwise, when you sell or replace one of them you may have to rewrite your will.

One solution is to describe the type of item you wish to give. For example, instead of saying, "I leave my 1998 Ford to my sister," you should say, "I leave any automobile I own at the time of my death to my sister."

Of course, if you do mean to give a specific item, you should describe it. For example instead of "I leave my diamond ring to Joan," you should say, "I leave to Joan the one-half carat diamond ring which I inherited from my grandmother," because you might own more than one diamond ring at the time of your death. (Hopefully!)

HANDWRITTEN
LIST OF
PERSONAL
PROPERTY

In Pennsylvania, you are allowed to leave a handwritten list of personal items (other than money or property used in a trade or business) that you wish to go to certain people and this would be legally binding. The wills in this book include a clause stating that you may leave such a list. This list must be signed by you. It may be made before or after your will and it may be changed at any time. It does not need to be witnessed. However, it should reflect your intention to dispose of these items in connection with your will. Otherwise, a court might interpret it to be a list of items you intended to give away while your were still living.

SPECIFIC BEQUESTS

Occasionally a person will want to leave a little something to a friend or charity and the rest to the family. This can be done with a *specific bequest* such as "$1,000 to my dear friend Martha Jones." Of course there could be a problem if, at the time of a person's death, there wasn't anything left after the specific bequests.

EXAMPLE

☞ At the time of making his will, Todd had $1,000,000 in assets. He felt generous so he left $50,000 to a local hospital, $50,000 to a local group that took care of homeless animals and the rest to his children. Unfortunately, several years later, the stock market crashed and he committed suicide by jumping off a bridge. His estate at the time was worth only $110,000 so after the above specific bequests and the legal fees and expenses of probate, there was nothing left for his five children.

Another problem with specific bequests is that some of the property may be worth considerably more or less at death than when the will was made.

EXAMPLE

☞ Joe wanted his two children to equally share his estate. His will left his son his stocks (worth $500,000 at the time) and his daughter $500,000 in cash. By the time of Joe's death the stock was only worth $100,000.

He should have left "fifty percent" of his estate to each child. If giving certain things to certain people is an important part of your estate plan, you can give specific items to specific persons, but remember to make changes if your assets change.

JOINT
BENEFICIARIES

Be careful about leaving one item of personal property to more than one person. For example, if you leave something to your son and his wife, what would happen if they divorce? Even if you leave something to two of your own children, what if they can't agree about who will have possession of it? Whenever possible, leave property to one person.

REMAINDER CLAUSE

One of the most important clauses in a will is the *remainder clause*. This is the clause that says something like "all the rest of my property I leave to…" This clause makes sure that the will disposes of all property owned at the time of death and that nothing is forgotten.

In a simple will, the best way to distribute property is to put it all in the remainder clause. In the first example in the previous section, the problem would have been avoided if the will had read as follows: "The rest, residue, and remainder of my estate I leave, five percent to ABC Hospital, five percent to XYZ Animal Welfare League and ninety percent to be divided equally among my children…"

ALTERNATE BENEFICIARIES

You should always provide for an *alternate beneficiary* in case the person you name dies before you and you do not have a chance to make out a new will.

SURVIVOR OR
DESCENDANTS

Suppose your will leaves your property to your sister and brother but your brother predeceases you. Should his share go to your sister or to your brother's children or grandchildren?

If you are giving property to two or more persons and if you want it all to go to the other if one of them dies, then you would specify "or the survivor of them."

If, on the other hand, you want the property to go to the children of the deceased person you should state in your will, "or their lineal descendants." This would include his or her children and grandchildren.

FAMILY OR
PERSON

If you decide you want it to go to your brother's children and grandchildren, you must next decide if an equal share should go to each family or to each person. For example, if your brother leaves three grandchildren, and one is an only child of his daughter and the others are the children of his son, should all grandchildren get equal shares, or should they take their parent's share?

When you want each family to get an equal share it is called *per stirpes*. When you want each person to get an equal share it is called *per capita*. Most of the wills in this book use per stirpes because that is the most common way property is left. If you wish to leave your property per capita then you can rewrite the will with this change.

EXAMPLE

☞ Alice leaves her property to her two daughters, Mary and Pat in equal shares, or to their lineal descendants per stirpes. Her daughter, Pat, predeceases Alice, leaving two children. Mary would receive one half of the estate and Pat's two children will receive the other half of the estate. In this case, if had Alice chosen per capita, Mary and the grandchildren would have each received one third of the estate.

Per Stirpes Distribution

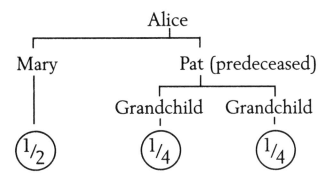

Per Capita Distribution

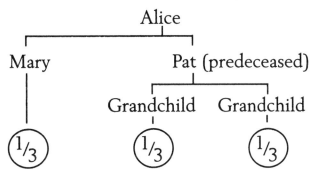

There are ten different simple will forms in this book, but you may want to divide your property slightly differently from what these forms state. If so, you can re-type the forms according to these rules, specifying whether the property should go to the survivor or the lineal descendants. If this is confusing to you, consider seeking the advice of an attorney.

SURVIVORSHIP

Many people put a clause in their will stating that anyone receiving property under the will must survive for thirty days (or forty-five or sixty) after the death of the deceased. This is so that if the two people die in the same accident there will not be two probates and the property will not go to the other party's heirs.

EXAMPLE ☞ Fred and Wilma were married and each had children by previous marriages. They didn't have survivorship clauses in their wills and they were in an airplane crash. Fred's children hired several expert witnesses and a large law firm to prove that at the time of the crash Fred lived for a few minutes longer than Wilma. That way when Wilma died first all of her property went to Fred. When he died a few minutes later, all of Fred and Wilma's property went to his children and Wilma's children received nothing.

GUARDIANS

If you have minor children you should name a guardian for them. There are two types of guardians, a guardian over the *person* and a guardian over the *property*. The first is the person who decides where the children will live and makes the other parental decisions for them. A guardian of the property is in charge of the minor's property and inheritance. In most cases, one person is appointed guardian of both the person and property. But some people prefer the children to live with one person, but to have the money held by another person.

EXAMPLE ☞ Sandra was a widow with a young daughter. She knew that if anything happened to her, her sister would be the best person to raise her daughter. But her sister was never good with money. So when Sandra made out her will, she named her sister as guardian over the person of her daughter and she named her father as guardian over the estate of her daughter.

When naming a guardian, it is always advisable to name an alternate guardian, in case your first choice is unable to serve for any reason.

CHILDREN'S TRUST

When a parent dies leaving a minor child and the child's property is held by a guardian, the guardianship ends when the child reaches the age of eighteen and all of the property is turned over to the child. Most parents do not feel their children are competent at the age of eighteen to handle large sums of money and prefer that it be held until the child is twenty-one, twenty-five, thirty or even older.

If you wish to set up a complicated system of deciding when your children should receive various amounts of your estate, you should consult a lawyer to draft a trust. However, if you want a simple provision that you want the funds held to a higher age than eighteen, and you have someone you trust to make decisions about paying for education or other expenses for your child or children, you can put that provision in your will as a children's trust.

The children's trust trustee can be the same person as the guardian or a different person. It is advisable to name an alternate trustee if your first choice is unable to handle it.

PERSONAL REPRESENTATIVE

A *personal representative* or *executor* is the person who will be in charge of your probate. He or she will gather your assets, handle the sale of them if necessary, prepare an inventory, hire an attorney, and distribute the property. It should be a person you trust and if it is, then you can state in your will that no bond is required to be posted by him or her. If the personal representative named in your will is a resident of Pennsylvania, no bond is required unless you request one in your will or it is ordered by the court. If the personal representative is not a Pennsylvania resident, you can state in your will that a bond is not required. In certain situations, the court may require that a surety bond be paid for by your estate to guaranty that the personal representative is honest. You can appoint a bank as your personal representative but their fees are usually very high.

It is best to have a Pennsylvania resident as a personal representative both because it is easier and because a bond may be required of a non-resident even if you state in your will that none is required.

Some people like to name two persons as personal representatives to avoid jealousy, or for other reasons. However, this is not a good idea. It makes double work in getting the papers signed and there can be problems if they cannot agree on something. You should, however, name an alternate personal representative in the event your first choice is unable to serve for any reason.

HANDWRITTEN WILLS

In Pennsylvania, a will that is entirely handwritten (called a *holographic* will) is also valid, even if there are no witnesses, but the material provisions of the will and the signature must be in your own handwriting. Since there is a greater chance a holographic will may be held invalid for some reason, it should only be used if you are in an emergency situation and are unable to find two persons to sign as witnesses.

WITNESSES

Unlike most states, a will does not have to be witnessed to be valid in Pennsylvania unless the testator signs the will with an "X" or another person signs the will for him. However, in order to probate a will in Pennsylvania, the will must be proved by the oaths of two witnesses. Proof by witnesses who signed the will is preferable. Although no witnesses are required to execute a typical will in Pennsylvania, it would be prudent to have at least two individuals witness and sign your will since Pennsylvania law prefers two signing witnesses to prove the will later in probate.

Contrary to popular belief, someone you leave property to *can* be a witness to your will. However, it is not a good idea, especially if there is anyone who may contest your will. It should only be done in dire emergencies.

Self-Proving Clause

Although a will requires no witnesses to be legal unless the testator makes his mark to the will or another person signs it for him, if the will is notarized and a self-proving clause is signed, it can be admitted to probate much faster. Without this clause, witnesses have to go to the courthouse and sign an oath. This can cause a delay in probating your estate if witnesses cannot get to the courthouse right away. With this clause it can be immediately accepted by the court even if both witnesses are dead.

Disinheriting Someone

Because it may result in your will being challenged in court, you should not make your own will if you intend to disinherit someone. However, you may wish to leave one child less than another because you already made a gift to that child, or perhaps that child needs the money less than the other.

If you do give more to one child than to another, then you should state your reasons to show that you thought out your plan. Otherwise, the one who got less might argue that you didn't realize what you were doing and were not competent to make a will.

FUNERAL ARRANGEMENTS

There is no harm in stating your funeral preferences in your will. However, directions for a funeral are not legally enforceable, and many times, a will is not found until after the funeral. Therefore it is better to tell your family about your wishes, make prior arrangements yourself, or leave a separate list of instructions.

FORMS

There are fourteen different will forms included in this book for easy use. You can either cut them out or photocopy them, or you can retype them on plain paper.

The forms in this book are printed on both sides of the page. If you photocopy them on separate pages or type your will on more than one piece of paper you should staple the pages together, initial each page and have both witnesses initial each page and each page should state at the bottom, "page 1 of 3," "page 2 of 3," etc.

CORRECTIONS

Your will should have no white-outs or erasures. If for some reason it is impossible to make a will without corrections, they should be initialed by you and both witnesses.

HOW TO EXECUTE A WILL 4

While most states require at least two witnesses to a will, Pennsylvania does not require any witnesses to a will that the testator signs. However, because of the requirements for probate and other state laws, it would be efficient estate planning to have at least two individuals witness and sign your will.

There are two important situations that require witnesses. First, if a testator is unable to sign his name for any reason, he may make his mark on the will and have his name written by another in his presence provided he makes his mark in the presence of two witnesses who sign their names to the will in his presence.

Second, if a testator is unable to sign his name or make his mark for any reason, another person may sign his name in his presence, and at his express direction, provided he declares the instrument to be his will in the presence of two witnesses who sign their names to his will in his presence.

The signing of a will is a serious legal event and must be done properly or the will may be declared invalid. Preferably it should be done in a private room without distraction. If witnesses are required as when the testator makes his mark on the will, all parties must watch each other sign and no one should leave the scene until all have signed.

EXAMPLE: ☞ Ebenezer was sick in bed and unable to sign his will. However, he was able to make his mark. Ebenezer's neighbor, John, then signed Ebenezer's name to the will in everyone's presence. George and Betty observed Ebenezer making his mark and signed their name to the will in his presence.

PROCEDURES: The person signing the will (the Testator) and the two witnesses should be able to see each other and the will. Two witnesses are suggested for ease of probate later on but are required if the testator is making his mark or someone is signing for him.

The Testator should state: "This is my will. I have read it and understand it and this is how I want it to read. I would like you two people to be the witnesses to my will." Then the testator and the witnesses should watch each other sign.

If the Testator cannot sign his name, someone else can sign his name in his presence either before or after he makes his mark. The two witnesses must witness the marking of the will and sign it in the Testator's presence.

If the Testator cannot sign his name or make his mark, he can direct someone else to sign for him in his presence by saying, "I am unable to mark or sign my will, I direct you, *(name of person)*, to sign it for me."

If there are multiple pages, the testator should initial the bottom of each page. Sign and date at the end of the will. Be sure that no language which is supposed to be part of the will appears after the testator's signature; such language may not be considered to be legally part of the will.

For a self-proved will a notary public should also be present and watch the signing. Then the parties should swear to the statements in the self-proving clause and sign again. Then the notary should sign and seal the will and write in the expiration date of his or her notary commission.

It is a good idea to make at least one copy of your will, but you should not sign or notarize the copies. The reason for this is if you cancel or intentionally destroy your original will, someone might bring out a copy and say that it is the original.

AFTER YOU SIGN YOUR WILL 5

STORING YOUR WILL

You should keep your will in a place safe from fire and easily accessible to your heirs. Your personal representative should know of its whereabouts. You can keep it in a home safe or fire box or in a safe deposit box in a bank. In some states, you should not place a will in a safe deposit box because they are sealed at death, but in Pennsylvania any person having possession or control of a will may be compelled by court order to deposit it with the court.

Wills are only filed after a person's death. No one has to know what you have put in your will while you are alive. Often an attorney preparing a will may offer to keep it in his safe deposit box at no charge. This is so that he or she will be contacted at the time of your death and be in a good position to do the necessary probate work.

REVOKING YOUR WILL

A person who has made a will may revoke it or may direct someone else to revoke it in his presence. You can revoke your will by burning, tearing, cancelling, obliterating or destroying it with the intention and for the purpose of revoking it. If any of these acts are done by someone at the direction and in the presence of the Testator, the oaths or affirmations of two witnesses are required to prove that the testator directed the individual to perform the act.

EXAMPLE: ☞ Ralph tells his son Clyde to go to the basement safe and tear up Ralph's will. If Clyde does not tear it up in Ralph's presence it is probably not effectively revoked.

REVIVAL   What if you change your will by drafting a new one and later decide you don't like the changes and want to go back to your old will? Can you destroy the new one and revive the old one? NO! Once you execute a new will revoking an old one you cannot revive the old one unless you execute a new document stating that you intend to revive the old will. In other words, you might as well execute a new will.

CHANGING YOUR WILL

After you sign your will you should not make changes to it. If you wish to change some provision of your will, you can do so by executing a document called a *codicil*. You may make an unlimited number of codicils to your will, but execute each one with the same formality of a will. Each should be self-proved, as well. It is usually better to prepare a new will than to prepare codicils.

If you wish to prepare a codicil to your will you can use form 18 included in this book in appendix B.

How to Make a 6 Living Will

No, a living will is not a videotape of a person making a will. It has nothing to do with the usual type of will that distributes property. A living will is a document by which a person declares that he or she does not want artificial life support systems used if he or she becomes incompetent and terminally ill. A person is considered incompetent if he lacks sufficient capacity to make or communicate decisions concerning himself.

Modern science can often keep a body alive even if the brain is permanently dead or if the person is in constant pain. In 1992, Pennsylvania passed a law that allowed a living will for the first time. Under this law, you can sign a living will at any time. It must be signed in front of two witnesses each of who are 18 years of age or older. If the person is physically unable to sign, he may direct an individual to sign it for him. However, an individual signing on your behalf cannot also sign as a witness.

Appendix B of this book includes a living will form; this is the form included in the Pennsylvania law. A living will does not have to be on that form to be legal. You can use a shorter version as long as it expresses the intention of the person to not have artificial life prolonging procedures used if he or she is incompetent and has a terminal condition. However, it is always best to use a statutory form than to make up your own. For more information on living wills, see *How to Make Your Own Living Will*, by Edward A. Haman, published by Sourcebooks, Inc.

How to Make Anatomical Gifts 7

Since 1972, Pennsylvania allows its residents to donate their bodies or organs for research or transplantation. The donation is called an *anatomical gift*. An individual making an anatomical gift must be of sound mind and 18 years of age or older. A relative of a deceased person may give consent but, because relatives are often in shock or too upset to make such a decision, it is better to have one's intent made clear before death. A statement in a will or another signed document such as a uniform donor card can clarify your intent. The gift may be all or part of one's body, and it may be made generally or to a specific person such as a physician or an ill relative. However, a gift of the whole body is not valid unless it is in writing at least fifteen days before the date of death.

You should sign the document making the donation before two witnesses who must also sign in each other's presence. If the donor cannot sign, the document may be signed for him at his direction in the presence of the witnesses.

The donor may designate in the document the physician who will carry out the procedure.

If the anatomical gift document has been delivered to a specific donee it may be amended or revoked by the donor in the following ways:

☞ By executing and delivering a signed statement to the donee.

☞ By an oral statement in the presence of two witnesses and communicated to the donee.

☞ By a statement made to an attending physician during a terminal illness or injury, and communicated to the donee.

☞ By a signed card or document found on the person of the donor or in his or her effects.

If a document of gift has not been delivered to a donee, you can revoke it by any of the above methods or by destruction, cancellation or mutilation of the document and all executed copies. You can also revoke it in the same manner a will is revoked as described on page 33.

Appendix B includes a uniform donor card as form 21. The individual donating the anatomical gift must be of sound mind and eighteen years of age or older. In addition, you must sign in the presence of two signing witnesses.

Appendix A
Sample Wills and Forms

The following pages include sample filled-in forms for some of the wills in this book. They are filled out in different ways for different situations. You should look at all of them to see how the different sections can be filled in. Only one example of a self-proved will affidavit is shown, but you should use it with every will.

Last Will and Testament

I, _____John Smith_____ a resident of _____Allegheny_____ County, Pennsylvania do hereby make, publish, and declare this to be my Last Will and Testament, hereby revoking any and all Wills and Codicils heretofore made by me.

FIRST: I direct that all my just debts and funeral expenses be paid out of my estate as soon after my death as is practicable.

SECOND: I may leave a statement or list disposing of certain items of my tangible personal property. Any such statement or list in existence at the time of my death shall be determinative with respect to all items bequeathed therein.

THIRD: I give, devise, and bequeath all my estate, real, personal, and mixed, of whatever kind and wherever situated, of which I may die seized or possessed, or in which I may have any interest or over which I may have any power of appointment or testamentary disposition, to my spouse, _____Barbara Smith_____. If my said spouse does not survive me, I give, and bequeath the said property to _my sisters, Jan Smith,_ _Joan Smith, and Jennifer Smith in equal shares-----------------------------------_ _---_, or the survivor of them.

FOURTH: In the event that any beneficiary fails to survive me by thirty days, then this will shall take effect as if that person had predeceased me.

FIFTH: I hereby nominate, constitute, and appoint _____Barbara Smith_____ as Personal Representative of this, my Last Will and Testament. In the event that such named person is unable or unwilling to serve at any time or for any reason, then I nominate, constitute, and appoint _____Reginald Smith_____ as Personal Representative in the place and stead of the person first named herein. It is my will and I direct that my Personal Representative shall not be required to furnish a bond for the faithful performance of his or her duties in any jurisdiction, any provision of law to the contrary notwithstanding, and I give my Personal Representative full power to administer my estate, including the power to settle claims, pay debts, and sell, lease or exchange real and personal property without court order.

IN WITNESS WHEREOF, I declare this to be my Last Will and Testament and execute it willingly as my free and voluntary act for the purposes expressed herein and I am of legal age and sound mind and make this under no constraint or undue influence, this _29th_ day of _January_, _2001_ at _Pittsburgh_ State of _Pennsylvania_.

_____John Smith_____ L.S.

The foregoing instrument was on said date subscribed at the end thereof by _____John Smith_____, the above named Testator who signed, published, and declared this instrument to be his/her Last Will and Testament in the presence of us and each of us, who thereupon at his/her request, in his/her presence, and in the presence of each other, have hereunto subscribed our names as witnesses thereto. We are of sound mind and proper age to witness a will and understand this to be his/her will, and to the best of our knowledge testator is of legal age to make a will, of sound mind, and under no constraint or undue influence.

_Brenda Jones_____ residing at___Pittsburgh, Pennsylvania_____

_John Doe_____ residing at___Pittsburgh, Pennsylvania_____

Last Will and Testament

I, _____John Smith_____ a resident of ___Montgomery___ County, Pennsylvania do hereby make, publish, and declare this to be my Last Will and Testament, hereby revoking any and all Wills and Codicils heretofore made by me.

FIRST: I direct that all my just debts and funeral expenses be paid out of my estate as soon after my death as is practicable.

SECOND: I may leave a statement or list disposing of certain items of my tangible personal property. Any such statement or list in existence at the time of my death shall be determinative with respect to all items bequeathed therein.

THIRD: I give, devise, and bequeath all my estate, real, personal, and mixed, of whatever kind and wherever situated, of which I may die seized or possessed, or in which I may have any interest or over which I may have any power of appointment or testamentary disposition, to my spouse, _____Barbara Smith_____. If my said spouse does not survive me, I give, and bequeath the said property to my children __Amy Smith, Beamy Smith, and Seamy Smith_____, in equal shares or to their lineal descendants, per stirpes.

FOURTH: In the event that any beneficiary fails to survive me by thirty days, then this will shall take effect as if that person had predeceased me.

FIFTH: I hereby nominate, constitute, and appoint _____Barbara Smith_____ as Personal Representative of this, my Last Will and Testament. In the event that such named person is unable or unwilling to serve at any time or for any reason, then I nominate, constitute, and appoint _____Reginald Smith_____ as Personal Representative in the place and stead of the person first named herein. It is my will and I direct that my Personal Representative shall not be required to furnish a bond for the faithful performance of his or her duties in any jurisdiction, any provision of law to the contrary notwithstanding, and I give my Personal Representative full power to administer my estate, including the power to settle claims, pay debts, and sell, lease or exchange real and personal property without court order.

IN WITNESS WHEREOF, I declare this to be my Last Will and Testament and execute it willingly as my free and voluntary act for the purposes expressed herein and I am of legal age and sound mind and make this under no constraint or undue influence, this __5th__ day of __January__, 2001 at ____Landsdale____ State of ____Pennsylvania__.

_____John Smith_____ L.S.

The foregoing instrument was on said date subscribed at the end thereof by
_____John Smith_____, the above named Testator who signed, pub-
lished, and declared this instrument to be his/her Last Will and Testament in the presence of
us and each of us, who thereupon at his/her request, in his/her presence, and in the presence
of each other, have hereunto subscribed our names as witnesses thereto. We are of sound
mind and proper age to witness a will and understand this to be his/her will, and to the best
of our knowledge testator is of legal age to make a will, of sound mind, and under no
constraint or undue influence.

_____Brenda Jones_____residing at____Pennsylvania_____

_____John Doe_____residing at____Pennsylvania_____

Last Will and Testament

I, _____John Doe_____ a resident of _____Lackawanna_____ County, Pennsylvania do hereby make, publish, and declare this to be my Last Will and Testament, hereby revoking any and all Wills and Codicils heretofore made by me.

FIRST: I direct that all my just debts and funeral expenses be paid out of my estate as soon after my death as is practicable.

SECOND: I may leave a statement or list disposing of certain items of my tangible personal property. Any such statement or list in existence at the time of my death shall be determinative with respect to all items bequeathed therein.

THIRD: I give, devise, and bequeath all my estate, real, personal, and mixed, of whatever kind and wherever situated, of which I may die seized or possessed, or in which I may have any interest or over which I may have any power of appointment or testamentary disposition, to my children _____James Doe, Mary Doe, Larry Doe, Barry Doe, Carrie Doe, and Moe Doe_____ plus any afterborn or adopted children in equal shares or to their lineal descendants per stirpes.

FOURTH: In the event that any beneficiary fails to survive me by thirty days, then this will shall take effect as if that person had predeceased me.

FIFTH: In the event any of my children have not attained the age of 18 years at the time of my death, I hereby nominate, constitute, and appoint _____Herbert Doe_____ as guardian over the person of any of my children who have not reached the age of majority at the time of my death. In the event that said guardian is unable or unwilling to serve, then I nominate, constitute, and appoint _____Tom Doe_____ as guardian. Said guardian shall serve without bond or surety.

SIXTH: In the event any of my children have not attained the age of 18 years at the time of my death, I hereby nominate, constitute, and appoint _____Herbert Doe_____ as guardian over the property of any of my children who have not reached the age of majority at the time of my death. In the event that said guardian is unable or unwilling to serve, then I nominate, constitute, and appoint _____Tom Doe_____ as guardian. Said guardian shall serve without bond or surety.

SEVENTH: I hereby nominate, constitute, and appoint _____Clarence Doe_____ as Personal Representative of this, my Last Will and Testament. In the event that such named person is unable or unwilling to serve at any time or for any reason, then I nominate, constitute, and appoint _____Englebert Doe_____ as Personal Representative in the place and stead of the person first named herein. It is my will and I direct that my Personal Representative shall not be required to furnish a bond for the faithful performance of his or her duties in any jurisdiction, any provision of law to the contrary notwithstanding, and I give my Personal Representative full power to administer my estate, including the power to settle claims, pay debts, and sell, lease or exchange real and personal property without court order.

IN WITNESS WHEREOF I declare this to be my Last Will and Testament and execute it willingly as my free and voluntary act for the purposes expressed herein and I am of legal age and sound mind and make this under no constraint or undue influence, this __2nd__ day of __July__, 2001 at __Scranton__ State of __Pennsylvania__.

_____ *John Doe* _____L.S.

The foregoing instrument was on said date subscribed at the end thereof by _____John Doe_____, the above named Testator who signed, published, and declared this instrument to be his/her Last Will and Testament in the presence of us and each of us, who thereupon at his/her request, in his/her presence, and in the presence of each other, have hereunto subscribed our names as witnesses thereto. We are of sound mind and proper age to witness a will and understand this to be his/her will, and to the best of our knowledge testator is of legal age to make a will, of sound mind, and under no constraint or undue influence.

_____*Jane Roe*_____residing at___Scranton, Pennsylvania___

_____*Melvin Coe*_____residing at___Scranton, Pennsylvania___

Last Will and Testament

I, _____Mary Smith_____ a resident of _Lackawanna_ County, Pennsylvania do hereby make, publish, and declare this to be my Last Will and Testament, hereby revoking any and all Wills and Codicils heretofore made by me.

FIRST: I direct that all my just debts and funeral expenses be paid out of my estate as soon after my death as is practicable.

SECOND: I may leave a statement or list disposing of certain items of my tangible personal property. Any such statement or list in existence at the time of my death shall be determinative with respect to all items bequeathed therein.

THIRD: I give, devise, and bequeath all my estate, real, personal, and mixed, of whatever kind and wherever situated, of which I may die seized or possessed, or in which I may have any interest or over which I may have any power of appointment or testamentary disposition, to the following: _my brothers John Smith and James Smith --------------_
_---_
_---_ , or to the survivor of them.

FOURTH: In the event that any beneficiary fails to survive me by thirty days, then this will shall take effect as if that person had predeceased me.

FIFTH: I hereby nominate, constitute, and appoint _Herbert Doe_ as Personal Representative of this, my Last Will and Testament. In the event that such named person is unable or unwilling to serve at any time or for any reason, then I nominate, constitute, and appoint _Tom Doe_ as Personal Representative in the place and stead of the person first named herein. It is my will and I direct that my Personal Representative shall not be required to furnish a bond for the faithful performance of his or her duties in any jurisdiction, any provision of law to the contrary notwithstanding, and I give my Personal Representative full power to administer my estate, including the power to settle claims, pay debts, and sell, lease or exchange real and personal property without court order.

IN WITNESS WHEREOF, I declare this to be my Last Will and Testament and execute it willingly as my free and voluntary act for the purposes expressed herein and I am of legal age and sound mind and make this under no constraint or undue influence, this _6th_ day of _May_ , _2002_ at _Scranton_ State of _Pennsylvania_ .

Mary Smith L.S.

The foregoing instrument was on said date subscribed at the end thereof by
_____Mary Smith_____, the above named Testator who signed, published, and declared this instrument to be his/her Last Will and Testament in the presence of us and each of us, who thereupon at his/her request, in his/her presence, and in the presence of each other, have hereunto subscribed our names as witnesses thereto. We are of sound mind and proper age to witness a will and understand this to be his/her will, and to the best of our knowledge testator is of legal age to make a will, of sound mind, and under no constraint or undue influence.

_____Leon Brown_____residing at___Scranton, Pennsylvania_____

_____Mildred Brown_____residing at___Scranton, Pennsylvania_____

Self-Proved Will Affidavit
(attach to Will)

COMMONWEALTH OF PENNSYLVANIA

COUNTY OF _____Lackawanna_____

    We, _____John Doe_____, _____Melvin Coe_____, and _____Jane Roe_____ the testator and the witnesses respectively, whose names are signed to the attached or foregoing instrument, having been sworn, declared to the undersigned officer that the testator, in the presence of witnesses, signed the instrument as his/her last will, that he/she signed willingly and executed the will as his/her free and voluntary act, that to the best of our knowledge the testator was at that time 18 years of age or older, of sound mind and under no constraint or undue influence, and that each of the witnesses, in the presence of the testator and in the presence of each other, signed the will as witnesses.

_____*John Doe*_____
Testator___John Doe___

_____*Jane Roe*_____
Witness___Jane Roe___

_____*Melvin Coe*_____
Witness___Melvin Coe___

    Subscribed and sworn to before me by ___John Doe___ the testator, and by _____Jane Roe_____ and _____Melvin Coe_____, the witnesses, all of whom personally appeared before me on ___July 5___, ___2001___. The testator, _____ is personally known to me or has produced___Pa.Dr. Lic. 12 345 678___ as identification, ___Jane Roe___ is personally known to me or has produced ___Pa.Dr. Lic. 45 678 901___ as identification ___Melvin Coe___ is personally known to me or has produced ___Pa.Dr. Lic. 98 765 432___ as identification.

_____*C.U. Sine*_____
Notary Public
My commission expires:
My commission number is:

(Notary Seal)

Codicil to the Will of

_____ Larry Lowe _____

I, _____ Larry Lowe _____, a resident of _____ Erie _____ County, Pennsylvania declare this to be the first codicil to my Last Will and Testament dated _____ July 5 _____, ___ 2001 ___.

FIRST: I hereby revoke the clause of my Will which reads as follows:
FOURTH: I hereby leave $5000.00 to my daughter Mildred-----------------------
----

-- .

SECOND: I hereby add the following clause to my Will: _____
FOURTH: I hereby leave $1000.00 to my daughter Mildred -----------------------
----

-- .

THIRD: In all other respects I hereby confirm and republish my Last Will and Testament dated _____ July 5 _____, ___ 2001 ___.

IN WITNESS WHEREOF, I have signed, published, and declared the foregoing instrument as and for a codicil to my Last Will and Testament, this ___ 5th ___ day of _____ January _____, ___ 2002 ___.

_____ _Larry Lowe_ _____

The foregoing instrument was on the _5th_ day of _____ January _____, ___ 2002 ___, signed at the end thereof, and at the same time published and declared by _____ Larry Lowe _____, as and for a codicil to his/her Last Will and Testament, dated _____ July 5 _____, ___ 2001 ___, in the presence of each of us, who, this attestation clause having been read to us, did at the request of the said testator/testatrix, in his/her presence and in the presence of each other sign our names as witnesses thereto.

James Smith _____ residing at _____ Erie, Pennsylvania _____

Mary Smith _____ residing at _____ Erie, Pennsylvania _____

Living Will

Declaration made this ___29___ day of _____January_____, __2002__. I, _____Norman Milquetoast_____, willfully and voluntarily make known my desire that my dying not be artificially prolonged under the circumstances set forth below, and I do hereby declare:

If at any time I have a terminal condition and if my attending or treating physician and another consulting physician have determined that there can be no medical probability of my recovery from such condition, I direct that life-prolonging procedures be withheld or withdrawn when the application of such procedures would serve only to prolong artificially the process of dying, and that I be permitted to die naturally with only the administration of medication or the performance of any medical procedure deemed necessary to provide me with comfort, care or alleviate pain.

It is my intention that this declaration be honored by my family and physician as the final expression of my legal right to refuse medical or surgical treatment and to accept the consequences for such refusal.

In the event that I have been determined to be unable to provide express and informed consent regarding the withholding, withdrawal, or continuation of life-prolonging procedures, I wish to designate, as my surrogate to carry out the provisions of this declaration:

Name: ___Betty Milquetoast_____

Address: ___1234 Pennsylvania Avenue_____

___Erie, Pennsylvania_____ Zip Code: ___16515_____

Phone: ___814-555-1212_____

I understand the full import of this declaration, and am emotionally and mentally competent to make this declaration.

Additional instructions (optional):

___----None --------_____

_____

_____*Norman Milquetoast*_____

(Signed)

_____*June Nabor*_____

Witness

___1236 Pennsylvania Avenue___

___Erie, PA 16515___

Address

___814-555-2121___

Phone

_____*Harvey Nabor*_____

Witness

___1236 Pennsylvania Avenue___

___Erie, PA 16515___

Address

___814-555-2121___

Phone

50

APPENDIX B
WILLS AND FORMS

The following pages contain forms that can be used to prepare a will, codicil, living will, and Uniform Donor Card. They should only be used by persons who have read this book, who do not have any complications in their legal affairs and who understand the forms they are using. The forms may be used right out of the book or they may be photocopied or retyped. Two copies of each form are included.

Form 1. Asset and Beneficiary List—*Use this form to keep an accurate record of your estate as well as your beneficiaries' names and addresses.*

Form 2. Preferences and Information List—*Use this form to let your family know of your wishes on matters not usually included in a will.*

Form 3. Simple Will—Spouse and Minor Children—One Guardian. *Use this will if you have minor children and want all your property to go to your spouse, but if your spouse dies previously, then to your minor children. It provides for one person to be guardian over your children and their estates.*

Form 4. Simple Will—Spouse and Minor Children—Two Guardians. *Use this will if you have minor children and want all your property to go to your spouse, but if your spouse dies previously, then to your minor children. It provides for two guardians, one over your children and one over their estates.*

Form 5. Simple Will—Spouse and Minor Children—Guardian and Trust. *This will should be used if you have minor children and want all your property to go to your spouse, but if your spouse dies previously, then to your minor children. It provides for one person to be guardian over your* *children and for either the same person or another to be trustee over their property. This will allows your children's property to be held until they are older than eighteen rather than distributing it all to them at age eighteen.*

Form 6. Simple Will—Spouse and No Children. *Use this will if you want your property to go to your spouse but if your spouse predeceases you, to others or the* **survivor** *of the others.*

Form 7. Simple Will—Spouse and No Children. *Use this will if you want your property to go to your spouse but if your spouse predeceases you, to others or the* **descendants** *of the others.*

Form 8. Simple Will—Spouse and Adult Children. *Use this will if you want all of your property to go to your spouse, but if your spouse dies previously, then to your children, all of whom are adults.*

Form 9. Simple Will—Spouse and Adult Children. *Use this will if you want some of your property to go to your spouse, and some of your property to your children, all of whom are adults.*

Form 10. Simple Will—No Spouse—Minor Children—One Guardian. *Use this will if you do not have a spouse and want all your property to go to your children, at least one of whom is a minor. It provides for one person to be guardian over your children and their estates.*

Form 11. Simple Will—No Spouse—Minor Children—Two Guardians. *Use this will if you do not have a spouse and want all your property to go to your children, at least one of whom is a minor. It provides for two guardians, one over your children and one over their estates.*

Form 12. Simple Will—No Spouse—Minor Children—Guardian and Trust. *Use this will if you do not have a spouse and want all your property to go to your children, at least one of whom is a minor. It provides for one person to be guardian over your children and for either that person or another to be trustee over their property. This will allows your children's property to be held until they are older than eighteen rather than distributing it all to them at age eighteen.*

Form 13. Simple Will—No Spouse—Adult Children. *This will should be used if you wish to leave your property to your adult children, or equally to each* **family** *if they predecease you.*

Form 14. Simple Will—No Spouse—Adult Children. *This will should be used if you wish to leave your property to your adult children, or equally to each* **person** *if they predecease you.*

Form 15. Simple Will—No Spouse and No Children. *Use this will if you have no spouse or children and want your property to go to the* **survivor** *of the people you name.*

Form 16. Simple Will—No Spouse and No Children. *Use this will if you have no spouse or children and want your property to go to the* **descendants** *of the people you name.*

Form 17. Self-Proved Will Page. *This page should be attached to every will as the last page. It must be witnessed and notarized.*

Form 18. Codicil to Will. *This form can be used to change one section of your will. Usually it is just as easy to execute a new will, since all of the same formalities are required.*

Form 19. Self-Proved Codicil Page. *If you decided to execute a codicil instead of making a new will, this page should be attached to your codicil as the last page. It must be witnessed and notarized.*

Form 20. Living Will. *This is a document which expresses your desire to withhold certain extraordinary medical treatment should you have a terminal illness and you reach such a state that your wishes to withhold such treatment cannot be determined.*

Form 21. Organ Donor Card. *This form is used to spell out your wishes for donation of your body or any organs.*

HOW TO PICK THE RIGHT WILL

Follow the chart and use the form number in the black circle,
then use Form 17, the self-proving affidavit.

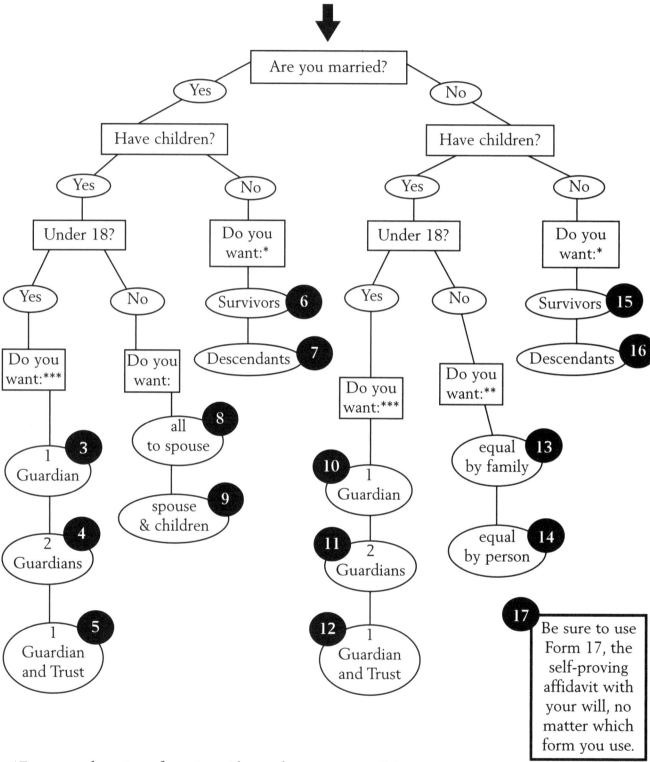

*For an explanation of survivors/descendants, see page 24.

**For an explanation of families/persons, see page 24.

*** For an explanation of children's guardians and trust, see pages 26-27

Asset and Beneficiary List

Property Inventory

Assets

Bank Accounts (checking, savings, certificates of deposit)

_____
_____
_____
_____
_____
_____
_____
_____

Real Estate

_____
_____
_____
_____
_____
_____
_____
_____

Vehicles (cars, trucks, boats, planes, RVs, etc.)

_____
_____
_____
_____
_____
_____
_____
_____

Personal Property (collections, jewelry, tools, artwork, household items, etc.)

_____
_____
_____
_____
_____
_____
_____

_____

_____

_____

_____

_____

_____

_____

_____

Stocks/Bonds/Mutual Funds

_____

_____

_____

_____

_____

_____

_____

_____

_____

_____

_____

_____

_____

_____

_____

Retirement Accounts (IRAs, 401(k)s, pension plans, etc.)

_____

_____

_____

_____

_____

_____

_____

Receivables (mortgages held, notes, accounts receivable, personal loans)

_____

_____

_____

_____

_____

Life Insurance

_____
_____
_____
_____
_____
_____
_____
_____

Other Property (trusts, partnerships, businesses, profit sharing, copyrights, etc.)

_____
_____
_____
_____
_____
_____
_____
_____

Liabilities

Real Estate Loans

_____
_____
_____
_____
_____
_____
_____

Vehicle Loans

_____
_____
_____
_____
_____
_____
_____
_____

Other Secured Loans

_____
_____
_____
_____
_____
_____
_____
_____

Unsecured Loans and Debts (taxes, child support, judgments, etc.)

_____
_____
_____
_____
_____
_____
_____

Beneficiary List

Name_____ Address_____ Phone_____

_____
_____
_____
_____
_____
_____
_____
_____

Preferences and Information List

STATEMENT OF DESIRES AND LOCATION OF PROPERTY & DOCUMENTS

I, _____, am signing this document as the expression of my desires as to the matters stated below, and to inform my family members or other significant persons of the location of certain property and documents in the event of any emergency or of my death.

1. **Funeral Desires.** It is my desire that the following arrangements be made for my funeral and disposition of remains in the event of my death (state if you have made any arrangements, such as pre-paid burial plans, cemetery plots owned, etc.):

    ❑ Burial at _____
    _____.

    ❑ Cremation at _____
    _____.

    ❑ Other specific desires: _____
    _____
    _____.

2. **Pets.** I have the following pet(s): _____
_____. The following are my desires concerning the care of said pet(s): _____
_____
_____.

4. **Notification.** I would like the following person(s) notified in the event of emergency or death (give name, address and phone number):

_____
_____
_____
_____
_____.

5. **Location of Documents.** The following is a list of important documents, and their location:

    ❑ Last Will and Testament, dated _____. Location: _____
    _____.

    ❑ Durable Power of Attorney, dated _____. Location: _____
    _____.

    ❑ Living Will, dated _____. Location: _____

    _____.

    ❑ Deed(s) to real estate (describe property location and location of deed):
    _____
    _____
    _____

❏ Title(s) to vehicles (cars, boats, etc.) (Describe vehicle, its location, and location of title, registration, or other documents):

_____
_____
_____
_____

❏ Life insurance policies (list name address & phone number of insurance company and insurance agent, policy number, and location of policy):

_____
_____
_____
_____

❏ Other insurance policies (list type, company & agent, policy number, and location of policy):

_____
_____
_____

❏ Other: (list other documents such as stock certificates, bonds, certificates of deposit, etc., and their location):

_____
_____
_____

6. **Location of Assets.** In addition to items readily visible in my home or listed above, I have the following assets:

❏ Safe deposit box located at _____, box number _____. Key located at: _____.

❏ Bank accounts (list name & address of bank, type of account, and account number):

_____

❏ Other (describe the item and give its location):

_____
_____
_____
_____
_____

7. Other desires or information (state any desires or provide any information not given above; use additional sheets of paper if necessary):

_____
_____
_____
_____
_____

Dated: _____

_____
Signature

Last Will and Testament

I, _____ a resident of _____ County, Pennsylvania do hereby make, publish, and declare this to be my Last Will and Testament, hereby revoking any and all Wills and Codicils heretofore made by me.

FIRST: I direct that all my just debts and funeral expenses be paid out of my estate as soon after my death as is practicable.

SECOND: I may leave a statement or list disposing of certain items of my tangible personal property. Any such statement or list in existence at the time of my death shall be determinative with respect to all items bequeathed therein.

THIRD: I give, devise, and bequeath all my estate, real, personal, and mixed, of whatever kind and wherever situated, of which I may die seized or possessed, or in which I may have any interest or over which I may have any power of appointment or testamentary disposition, to my spouse, _____. If my said spouse does not survive me, I give, devise and bequeath the said property to my children _____

_____

_____,

plus any afterborn or adopted children in equal shares or their lineal descendants, per stirpes.

FOURTH: In the event that any beneficiary fails to survive me by thirty days, then this will shall take effect as if that person had predeceased me.

FIFTH: Should my spouse not survive me, I hereby nominate, constitute, and appoint _____ as guardian over the person and estate of any of my children who have not reached the age of majority at the time of my death. In the event that said guardian is unable or unwilling to serve, then I nominate, constitute, and appoint _____ as guardian. Said guardian shall serve without bond or surety.

SIXTH: I hereby nominate, constitute, and appoint _____ as Personal Representative of this, my Last Will and Testament. In the event that such named person is unable or unwilling to serve at any time or for any reason, then I nominate, constitute, and appoint _____ as Personal Representative in the place and stead of the person first named herein. It is my will and I direct that my Personal Representative shall not be required to furnish a bond for the faithful performance of his or her duties in any jurisdiction, any provision of law to the contrary notwithstanding, and I give my Personal Representative full power to administer my estate, including the power to settle claims, pay debts, and sell, lease or exchange real and personal property without court order.

IN WITNESS WHEREOF, I declare this to be my Last Will and Testament and execute it willingly as my free and voluntary act for the purposes expressed herein and I am of legal age and sound mind and make this under no constraint or undue influence, this _____ day of _____, _____ at _____ State of _____.

_____L.S.

The foregoing instrument was on said date subscribed at the end thereof by _____, the above named Testator who signed, published, and declared this instrument to be his/her Last Will and Testament in the presence of us and each of us, who thereupon at his/her request, in his/her presence, and in the presence of each other, have hereunto subscribed our names as witnesses thereto. We are of sound mind and proper age to witness a will and understand this to be his/her will, and to the best of our knowledge testator is of legal age to make a will, of sound mind, and under no constraint or undue influence.

_____residing at_____

_____residing at_____

Last Will and Testament

I, _____ a resident of _____ County, Pennsylvania do hereby make, publish, and declare this to be my Last Will and Testament, hereby revoking any and all Wills and Codicils heretofore made by me.

FIRST: I direct that all my just debts and funeral expenses be paid out of my estate as soon after my death as is practicable.

SECOND: I may leave a statement or list disposing of certain items of my tangible personal property. Any such statement or list in existence at the time of my death shall be determinative with respect to all items bequeathed therein.

THIRD: I give, devise, and bequeath all my estate, real, personal, and mixed, of whatever kind and wherever situated, of which I may die seized or possessed, or in which I may have any interest or over which I may have any power of appointment or testamentary disposition, to my spouse, _____. If my said spouse does not survive me, I give, devise and bequeath the said property to my children _____ _____ _____, plus any afterborn or adopted children in equal shares or their lineal descendants, per stirpes.

FOURTH: In the event that any beneficiary fails to survive me by thirty days, then this will shall take effect as if that person had predeceased me.

FIFTH: Should my spouse not survive me, I hereby nominate, constitute, and appoint _____, as guardian over the person of any of my children who have not reached the age of majority at the time of my death. In the event that said guardian is unable or unwilling to serve, then I nominate, constitute, and appoint _____ as guardian. Any guardian shall serve without bond or surety.

SIXTH: Should my spouse not survive me, I hereby nominate, constitute, and appoint _____ as guardian over the estate of any of my children who have not reached the age of majority at the time of my death. In the event that said guardian is unable or unwilling to serve, then I nominate, constitute, and appoint _____ _____as guardian. Any guardian shall serve without bond or surety.

SEVENTH: I hereby nominate, constitute, and appoint _____ as Personal Representative of this, my Last Will and Testament. In the event that such named person is unable or unwilling to serve at any time or for any reason, then I nominate, constitute, and appoint _____ as Personal Representative in the place and stead of the person first named herein. It is my will and I direct that my Personal Representative shall not be required to furnish a bond for the faithful performance of his or her duties in any jurisdiction, any provision of law to the contrary notwithstanding, and I give my Personal Representative full power to administer my estate, including the power to settle claims, pay debts, and sell, lease or exchange real and personal property without court order.

IN WITNESS WHEREOF, I declare this to be my Last Will and Testament and execute it willingly as my free and voluntary act for the purposes expressed herein and I am of legal age and sound mind and make this under no constraint or undue influence, this _____ day of _____, _____ at _____ State of _____.

_____L.S.

The foregoing instrument was on said date subscribed at the end thereof by _____, the above named Testator who signed, published, and declared this instrument to be his/her Last Will and Testament in the presence of us and each of us, who thereupon at his/her request, in his/her presence, and in the presence of each other, have hereunto subscribed our names as witnesses thereto. We are of sound mind and proper age to witness a will and understand this to be his/her will, and to the best of our knowledge testator is of legal age to make a will, of sound mind, and under no constraint or undue influence.

_____residing at_____

_____residing at_____

Last Will and Testament

I, _____ a resident of _____ County, Pennsylvania do hereby make, publish, and declare this to be my Last Will and Testament, hereby revoking any and all Wills and Codicils heretofore made by me.

FIRST: I direct that all my just debts and funeral expenses be paid out of my estate as soon after my death as is practicable.

SECOND: I may leave a statement or list disposing of certain items of my tangible personal property. Any such statement or list in existence at the time of my death shall be determinative with respect to all items bequeathed therein.

THIRD: I give, devise, and bequeath all my estate, real, personal, and mixed, of whatever kind and wherever situated, of which I may die seized or possessed, or in which I may have any interest or over which I may have any power of appointment or testamentary disposition, to my spouse, _____. If my said spouse does not survive me, I give, devise and bequeath the said property to my children _____

_____

_____,

plus any afterborn or adopted children in equal shares or their lineal descendants, per stirpes.

FOURTH: In the event that any beneficiary fails to survive me by thirty days, then this will shall take effect as if that person had predeceased me.

FIFTH: In the event that any of my children have not reached the age of _____ years at the time of my death, then the share of any such child shall be held in a separate trust by _____ for such child.

The trustee shall use the income and that part of the principal of the trust as is, in the trustee's sole discretion, necessary or desirable to provide proper housing, medical care, food, clothing, entertainment and education for the trust beneficiary, considering the beneficiary's other resources. Any income that is not distributed shall be added to the principal. Additionally, the trustee shall have all powers conferred by the law of the state having jurisdiction over this trust, as well as the power to pay from the assets of the trust reasonable fees necessary to administer the trust.

The trust shall terminate when the child reaches the age specified above and the remaining assets distributed to the child, unless they have been exhausted sooner. In the event the child dies prior to the termination of the trust, then the assets shall pass to the estate of the child. The interests of the beneficiary under this trust shall not be assignable and shall be free from the claims of creditors to the full extent allowed by law.

In the event the said trustee is unable or unwilling to serve for any reason, then I nominate, constitute, and appoint _____ as alternate trustee.

No bond shall be required of either trustee in any jurisdiction and this trust shall be administered without court supervision as allowed by law.

SIXTH: Should my spouse not survive me, I hereby nominate, constitute, and appoint _____as guardian over the person and estate of any of my children who have not reached the age of majority at the time of my death. In the event that said guardian is unable or unwilling to serve, then I nominate, constitute, and appoint _____ as guardian. Any guardian shall serve without bond or surety.

SEVENTH: I hereby nominate, constitute, and appoint _____ as Personal Representative of this, my Last Will and Testament. In the event that such named person is unable or unwilling to serve at any time or for any reason, then I nominate, constitute, and appoint _____ as Personal Representative in the place and stead of the person first named herein. It is my will and I direct that my Personal Representative shall not be required to furnish a bond for the faithful performance of his or her duties in any jurisdiction, any provision of law to the contrary notwithstanding, and I give my Personal Representative full power to administer my estate, including the power to settle claims, pay debts, and sell, lease or exchange real and personal property without court order.

IN WITNESS WHEREOF, I declare this to be my Last Will and Testament and execute it willingly as my free and voluntary act for the purposes expressed herein and I am of legal age and sound mind and make this under no constraint or undue influence, this _____ day of _____, _____ at _____ State of _____.

_____L.S.

The foregoing instrument was on said date subscribed at the end thereof by _____, the above named Testator who signed, published, and declared this instrument to be his/her Last Will and Testament in the presence of us and each of us, who thereupon at his/her request, in his/her presence, and in the presence of each other, have hereunto subscribed our names as witnesses thereto. We are of sound mind and proper age to witness a will and understand this to be his/her will, and to the best of our knowledge testator is of legal age to make a will, of sound mind, and under no constraint or undue influence.

_____residing at_____

_____residing at_____

Last Will and Testament

I, _____ a resident of _____ County, Pennsylvania do hereby make, publish, and declare this to be my Last Will and Testament, hereby revoking any and all Wills and Codicils heretofore made by me.

FIRST: I direct that all my just debts and funeral expenses be paid out of my estate as soon after my death as is practicable.

SECOND: I may leave a statement or list disposing of certain items of my tangible personal property. Any such statement or list in existence at the time of my death shall be determinative with respect to all items bequeathed therein.

THIRD: I give, devise, and bequeath all my estate, real, personal, and mixed, of whatever kind and wherever situated, of which I may die seized or possessed, or in which I may have any interest or over which I may have any power of appointment or testamentary disposition, to my spouse, _____. If my said spouse does not survive me, I give, devise and bequeath the said property to _____ _____ _____,

or the survivor of them.

FOURTH: In the event that any beneficiary fails to survive me by thirty days, then this will shall take effect as if that person had predeceased me.

FIFTH: I hereby nominate, constitute, and appoint _____ as Personal Representative of this, my Last Will and Testament. In the event that such named person is unable or unwilling to serve at any time or for any reason, then I nominate, constitute, and appoint _____ as Personal Representative in the place and stead of the person first named herein. It is my will and I direct that my Personal Representative shall not be required to furnish a bond for the faithful performance of his or her duties in any jurisdiction, any provision of law to the contrary notwithstanding, and I give my Personal Representative full power to administer my estate, including the power to settle claims, pay debts, and sell, lease or exchange real and personal property without court order.

IN WITNESS WHEREOF, I declare this to be my Last Will and Testament and execute it willingly as my free and voluntary act for the purposes expressed herein and I am of legal age and sound mind and make this under no constraint or undue influence, this _____ day of _____, _____ at _____ State of _____.

_____L.S.

The foregoing instrument was on said date subscribed at the end thereof by
_____, the above named Testator who signed, published, and declared this instrument to be his/her Last Will and Testament in the presence of us and each of us, who thereupon at his/her request, in his/her presence, and in the presence of each other, have hereunto subscribed our names as witnesses thereto. We are of sound mind and proper age to witness a will and understand this to be his/her will, and to the best of our knowledge testator is of legal age to make a will, of sound mind, and under no constraint or undue influence.

_____residing at_____

_____residing at_____

Last Will and Testament

I, _____ a resident of _____ County, Pennsylvania do hereby make, publish, and declare this to be my Last Will and Testament, hereby revoking any and all Wills and Codicils heretofore made by me.

FIRST: I direct that all my just debts and funeral expenses be paid out of my estate as soon after my death as is practicable.

SECOND: I may leave a statement or list disposing of certain items of my tangible personal property. Any such statement or list in existence at the time of my death shall be determinative with respect to all items bequeathed therein.

THIRD: I give, devise, and bequeath all my estate, real, personal, and mixed, of whatever kind and wherever situated, of which I may die seized or possessed, or in which I may have any interest or over which I may have any power of appointment or testamentary disposition, to my spouse, _____. If my said spouse does not survive me, I give, devise and bequeath the said property to _____ _____ _____, or to their lineal descendants, per stirpes.

FOURTH: In the event that any beneficiary fails to survive me by thirty days, then this will shall take effect as if that person had predeceased me.

FIFTH: I hereby nominate, constitute, and appoint _____ as Personal Representative of this, my Last Will and Testament. In the event that such named person is unable or unwilling to serve at any time or for any reason, then I nominate, constitute, and appoint _____ as Personal Representative in the place and stead of the person first named herein. It is my will and I direct that my Personal Representative shall not be required to furnish a bond for the faithful performance of his or her duties in any jurisdiction, any provision of law to the contrary notwithstanding, and I give my Personal Representative full power to administer my estate, including the power to settle claims, pay debts, and sell, lease or exchange real and personal property without court order.

IN WITNESS WHEREOF, I declare this to be my Last Will and Testament and execute it willingly as my free and voluntary act for the purposes expressed herein and I am of legal age and sound mind and make this under no constraint or undue influence, this _____ day of _____, _____ at _____ State of _____.

_____L.S.

The foregoing instrument was on said date subscribed at the end thereof by _____, the above named Testator who signed, published, and declared this instrument to be his/her Last Will and Testament in the presence of us and each of us, who thereupon at his/her request, in his/her presence, and in the presence of each other, have hereunto subscribed our names as witnesses thereto. We are of sound mind and proper age to witness a will and understand this to be his/her will, and to the best of our knowledge testator is of legal age to make a will, of sound mind, and under no constraint or undue influence.

_____residing at_____

_____residing at_____

Last Will and Testament

I, _____ a resident of _____ County, Pennsylvania do hereby make, publish, and declare this to be my Last Will and Testament, hereby revoking any and all Wills and Codicils heretofore made by me.

FIRST: I direct that all my just debts and funeral expenses be paid out of my estate as soon after my death as is practicable.

SECOND: I may leave a statement or list disposing of certain items of my tangible personal property. Any such statement or list in existence at the time of my death shall be determinative with respect to all items bequeathed therein.

THIRD: I give, devise, and bequeath all my estate, real, personal, and mixed, of whatever kind and wherever situated, of which I may die seized or possessed, or in which I may have any interest or over which I may have any power of appointment or testamentary disposition, to my spouse, _____. If my said spouse does not survive me, I give, devise and bequeath the said property to my children

_____

_____,

in equal shares or to their lineal descendants, per stirpes.

FOURTH: In the event that any beneficiary fails to survive me by thirty days, then this will shall take effect as if that person had predeceased me.

FIFTH: I hereby nominate, constitute, and appoint _____ as Personal Representative of this, my Last Will and Testament. In the event that such named person is unable or unwilling to serve at any time or for any reason, then I nominate, constitute, and appoint _____ as Personal Representative in the place and stead of the person first named herein. It is my will and I direct that my Personal Representative shall not be required to furnish a bond for the faithful performance of his or her duties in any jurisdiction, any provision of law to the contrary notwithstanding, and I give my Personal Representative full power to administer my estate, including the power to settle claims, pay debts, and sell, lease or exchange real and personal property without court order.

IN WITNESS WHEREOF, I declare this to be my Last Will and Testament and execute it willingly as my free and voluntary act for the purposes expressed herein and I am of legal age and sound mind and make this under no constraint or undue influence, this _____ day of _____, _____ at _____ State of _____.

_____L.S.

The foregoing instrument was on said date subscribed at the end thereof by _____, the above named Testator who signed, published, and declared this instrument to be his/her Last Will and Testament in the presence of us and each of us, who thereupon at his/her request, in his/her presence, and in the presence of each other, have hereunto subscribed our names as witnesses thereto. We are of sound mind and proper age to witness a will and understand this to be his/her will, and to the best of our knowledge testator is of legal age to make a will, of sound mind, and under no constraint or undue influence.

_____residing at_____

_____residing at_____

Last Will and Testament

I, _____ a resident of _____ County, Pennsylvania do hereby make, publish, and declare this to be my Last Will and Testament, hereby revoking any and all Wills and Codicils heretofore made by me.

FIRST: I direct that all my just debts and funeral expenses be paid out of my estate as soon after my death as is practicable.

SECOND: I may leave a statement or list disposing of certain items of my tangible personal property. Any such statement or list in existence at the time of my death shall be determinative with respect to all items bequeathed therein.

THIRD: I give, devise, and bequeath all my estate, real, personal, and mixed, of whatever kind and wherever situated, of which I may die seized or possessed, or in which I may have any interest or over which I may have any power of appointment or testamentary disposition, as follows:

_____% to my spouse, _____ and

_____% to my children, _____

_____

_____,

in equal shares or to their lineal descendants per stirpes.

FOURTH: In the event that any beneficiary fails to survive me by thirty days, then this will shall take effect as if that person had predeceased me.

FIFTH: I hereby nominate, constitute, and appoint _____ as Personal Representative of this, my Last Will and Testament. In the event that such named person is unable or unwilling to serve at any time or for any reason, then I nominate, constitute, and appoint _____ as Personal Representative in the place and stead of the person first named herein. It is my will and I direct that my Personal Representative shall not be required to furnish a bond for the faithful performance of his or her duties in any jurisdiction, any provision of law to the contrary notwithstanding, and I give my Personal Representative full power to administer my estate, including the power to settle claims, pay debts, and sell, lease or exchange real and personal property without court order.

IN WITNESS WHEREOF, I declare this to be my Last Will and Testament and execute it willingly as my free and voluntary act for the purposes expressed herein and I am of legal age and sound mind and make this under no constraint or undue influence, this _____ day of _____, _____ at _____ State of _____.

_____L.S.

The foregoing instrument was on said date subscribed at the end thereof by _____, the above named Testator who signed, published, and declared this instrument to be his/her Last Will and Testament in the presence of us and each of us, who thereupon at his/her request, in his/her presence, and in the presence of each other, have hereunto subscribed our names as witnesses thereto. We are of sound mind and proper age to witness a will and understand this to be his/her will, and to the best of our knowledge testator is of legal age to make a will, of sound mind, and under no constraint or undue influence.

_____residing at_____

_____residing at_____

Last Will and Testament

I, _____ a resident of _____ County, Pennsylvania do hereby make, publish, and declare this to be my Last Will and Testament, hereby revoking any and all Wills and Codicils heretofore made by me.

FIRST: I direct that all my just debts and funeral expenses be paid out of my estate as soon after my death as is practicable.

SECOND: I may leave a statement or list disposing of certain items of my tangible personal property. Any such statement or list in existence at the time of my death shall be determinative with respect to all items bequeathed therein.

THIRD: I give, devise, and bequeath all my estate, real, personal, and mixed, of whatever kind and wherever situated, of which I may die seized or possessed, or in which I may have any interest or over which I may have any power of appointment or testamentary disposition, to my children _____

_____

_____,

plus any afterborn or adopted children in equal shares or to their lineal descendants per stirpes.

FOURTH: In the event that any beneficiary fails to survive me by thirty days, then this will shall take effect as if that person had predeceased me.

FIFTH: In the event any of my children have not attained the age of 18 years at the time of my death, I hereby nominate, constitute, and appoint _____ as guardian over the person and estate of any of my children who have not reached the age of majority at the time of my death. In the event that said guardian is unable or unwilling to serve, then I nominate, constitute, and appoint _____ as guardian. Any guardian shall serve without bond or surety.

SIXTH: I hereby nominate, constitute, and appoint _____ as Personal Representative of this, my Last Will and Testament. In the event that such named person is unable or unwilling to serve at any time or for any reason, then I nominate, constitute, and appoint _____ as Personal Representative in the place and stead of the person first named herein. It is my will and I direct that my Personal Representative shall not be required to furnish a bond for the faithful performance of his or her duties in any jurisdiction, any provision of law to the contrary notwithstanding, and I give my Personal Representative full power to administer my estate, including the power to settle claims, pay debts, and sell, lease or exchange real and personal property without court order.

IN WITNESS WHEREOF, I declare this to be my Last Will and Testament and execute it willingly as my free and voluntary act for the purposes expressed herein and I am of legal age and sound mind and make this under no constraint or undue influence, this _____ day of _____, _____ at _____ State of _____.

_____L.S.

The foregoing instrument was on said date subscribed at the end thereof by _____, the above named Testator who signed, published, and declared this instrument to be his/her Last Will and Testament in the presence of us and each of us, who thereupon at his/her request, in his/her presence, and in the presence of each other, have hereunto subscribed our names as witnesses thereto. We are of sound mind and proper age to witness a will and understand this to be his/her will, and to the best of our knowledge testator is of legal age to make a will, of sound mind, and under no constraint or undue influence.

_____residing at_____

_____residing at_____

Last Will and Testament

I, _____ a resident of _____ County, Pennsylvania do hereby make, publish, and declare this to be my Last Will and Testament, hereby revoking any and all Wills and Codicils heretofore made by me.

FIRST: I direct that all my just debts and funeral expenses be paid out of my estate as soon after my death as is practicable.

SECOND: I may leave a statement or list disposing of certain items of my tangible personal property. Any such statement or list in existence at the time of my death shall be determinative with respect to all items bequeathed therein.

THIRD: I give, devise, and bequeath all my estate, real, personal, and mixed, of whatever kind and wherever situated, of which I may die seized or possessed, or in which I may have any interest or over which I may have any power of appointment or testamentary disposition, to my children _____

_____

_____,

plus any afterborn or adopted children in equal shares or to their lineal descendants per stirpes.

FOURTH: In the event that any beneficiary fails to survive me by thirty days, then this will shall take effect as if that person had predeceased me.

FIFTH: In the event any of my children have not attained the age of 18 years at the time of my death, I hereby nominate, constitute, and appoint _____ as guardian over the person of any of my children who have not reached the age of majority at the time of my death. In the event that said guardian is unable or unwilling to serve, then I nominate, constitute, and appoint _____ as guardian. Any guardian shall serve without bond or surety.

SIXTH: In the event any of my children have not attained the age of 18 years at the time of my death, I hereby nominate, constitute, and appoint _____ as guardian over the estate of any of my children who have not reached the age of majority at the time of my death. In the event that said guardian is unable or unwilling to serve, then I nominate, constitute, and appoint _____ as guardian. Any guardian shall serve without bond or surety.

SEVENTH: I hereby nominate, constitute, and appoint _____ as Personal Representative of this, my Last Will and Testament. In the event that such named person is unable or unwilling to serve at any time or for any reason, then I nominate, constitute, and appoint _____ as Personal Representative in the place and stead of the person first named herein. It is my will and I direct that my Personal Representative shall not be required to furnish a bond for the faithful performance of his or her duties in any jurisdiction, any provision of law to the contrary notwithstanding, and I give my Personal Representative full power to administer my estate, including the power to settle claims, pay debts, and sell, lease or exchange real and personal property without court order.

IN WITNESS WHEREOF, I declare this to be my Last Will and Testament and execute it willingly as my free and voluntary act for the purposes expressed herein and I am of legal age and sound mind and make this under no constraint or undue influence, this _____ day of _____, _____ at _____ State of _____.

_____L.S.

The foregoing instrument was on said date subscribed at the end thereof by _____, the above named Testator who signed, published, and declared this instrument to be his/her Last Will and Testament in the presence of us and each of us, who thereupon at his/her request, in his/her presence, and in the presence of each other, have hereunto subscribed our names as witnesses thereto. We are of sound mind and proper age to witness a will and understand this to be his/her will, and to the best of our knowledge testator is of legal age to make a will, of sound mind, and under no constraint or undue influence.

_____residing at_____

_____residing at_____

Last Will and Testament

I, _____ a resident of _____ County, Pennsylvania do hereby make, publish, and declare this to be my Last Will and Testament, hereby revoking any and all Wills and Codicils heretofore made by me.

FIRST: I direct that all my just debts and funeral expenses be paid out of my estate as soon after my death as is practicable.

SECOND: I may leave a statement or list disposing of certain items of my tangible personal property. Any such statement or list in existence at the time of my death shall be determinative with respect to all items bequeathed therein.

THIRD: I give, devise, and bequeath all my estate, real, personal, and mixed, of whatever kind and wherever situated, of which I may die seized or possessed, or in which I may have any interest or over which I may have any power of appointment or testamentary disposition, to my children _____

_____

_____,

plus any afterborn or adopted children in equal shares or to their lineal descendants per stirpes.

FOURTH: In the event that any beneficiary fails to survive me by thirty days, then this will shall take effect as if that person had predeceased me.

FIFTH: In the event that any of my children have not reached the age of _____ years at the time of my death, then the share of any such child shall be held in a separate trust by _____ for such child.

The trustee shall use the income and that part of the principal of the trust as is, in the trustee's sole discretion, necessary or desirable to provide proper housing, medical care, food, clothing, entertainment and education for the trust beneficiary, considering the beneficiary's other resources. Any income that is not distributed shall be added to the principal. Additionally, the trustee shall have all powers conferred by the law of the state having jurisdiction over this trust, as well as the power to pay from the assets of the trust reasonable fees necessary to administer the trust.

The trust shall terminate when the child reaches the age specified above and the remaining assets distributed to the child, unless they have been exhausted sooner. In the event the child dies prior to the termination of the trust, then the assets shall pass to the estate of the child. The interests of the beneficiary under this trust shall not be assignable and shall be free from the claims of creditors to the full extent allowed by law.

In the event the said trustee is unable or unwilling to serve for any reason, then I nominate, constitute, and appoint _____as alternate trustee.

No bond shall be required of either trustee in any jurisdiction and this trust shall be administered without court supervision as allowed by law.

SIXTH: In the event any of my children have not attained the age of 18 years at the time of my death, I hereby nominate, constitute, and appoint _____ as guardian over the person and estate of any of my children who have not reached the age of majority at the time of my death. In the event that said guardian is unable or unwilling to serve, then I nominate, constitute, and appoint _____ as guardian. Any guardian shall serve without bond or surety.

SEVENTH: I hereby nominate, constitute, and appoint _____ as Personal Representative of this, my Last Will and Testament. In the event that such named person is unable or unwilling to serve at any time or for any reason, then I nominate, constitute, and appoint _____ as Personal Representative in the place and stead of the person first named herein. It is my will and I direct that my Personal Representative shall not be required to furnish a bond for the faithful performance of his or her duties in any jurisdiction, any provision of law to the contrary notwithstanding, and I give my Personal Representative full power to administer my estate, including the power to settle claims, pay debts, and sell, lease or exchange real and personal property without court order.

IN WITNESS WHEREOF, I declare this to be my Last Will and Testament and execute it willingly as my free and voluntary act for the purposes expressed herein and I am of legal age and sound mind and make this under no constraint or undue influence, this _____ day of _____, _____ at _____ State of _____.

_____L.S.

The foregoing instrument was on said date subscribed at the end thereof by _____, the above named Testator who signed, published, and declared this instrument to be his/her Last Will and Testament in the presence of us and each of us, who thereupon at his/her request, in his/her presence, and in the presence of each other, have hereunto subscribed our names as witnesses thereto. We are of sound mind and proper age to witness a will and understand this to be his/her will, and to the best of our knowledge testator is of legal age to make a will, of sound mind, and under no constraint or undue influence.

_____residing at_____

_____residing at_____

Last Will and Testament

I, _____ a resident of _____ County, Pennsylvania do hereby make, publish, and declare this to be my Last Will and Testament, hereby revoking any and all Wills and Codicils heretofore made by me.

FIRST: I direct that all my just debts and funeral expenses be paid out of my estate as soon after my death as is practicable.

SECOND: I may leave a statement or list disposing of certain items of my tangible personal property. Any such statement or list in existence at the time of my death shall be determinative with respect to all items bequeathed therein.

THIRD: I give, devise, and bequeath all my estate, real, personal, and mixed, of whatever kind and wherever situated, of which I may die seized or possessed, or in which I may have any interest or over which I may have any power of appointment or testamentary disposition, to my children _____

_____

_____,

in equal shares, or their lineal descendants per stirpes.

FOURTH: In the event that any beneficiary fails to survive me by thirty days, then this will shall take effect as if that person had predeceased me.

FIFTH: I hereby nominate, constitute, and appoint _____ as Personal Representative of this, my Last Will and Testament. In the event that such named person is unable or unwilling to serve at any time or for any reason, then I nominate, constitute, and appoint _____ as Personal Representative in the place and stead of the person first named herein. It is my will and I direct that my Personal Representative shall not be required to furnish a bond for the faithful performance of his or her duties in any jurisdiction, any provision of law to the contrary notwithstanding, and I give my Personal Representative full power to administer my estate, including the power to settle claims, pay debts, and sell, lease or exchange real and personal property without court order.

IN WITNESS WHEREOF, I declare this to be my Last Will and Testament and execute it willingly as my free and voluntary act for the purposes expressed herein and I am of legal age and sound mind and make this under no constraint or undue influence, this _____ day of _____, _____ at _____ State of _____.

_____L.S.

The foregoing instrument was on said date subscribed at the end thereof by
_____, the above named Testator who signed, published, and declared this instrument to be his/her Last Will and Testament in the presence of us and each of us, who thereupon at his/her request, in his/her presence, and in the presence of each other, have hereunto subscribed our names as witnesses thereto. We are of sound mind and proper age to witness a will and understand this to be his/her will, and to the best of our knowledge testator is of legal age to make a will, of sound mind, and under no constraint or undue influence.

_____residing at_____

_____residing at_____

Last Will and Testament

I, _____ a resident of _____
County, Pennsylvania do hereby make, publish, and declare this to be my Last Will and
Testament, hereby revoking any and all Wills and Codicils heretofore made by me.

FIRST: I direct that all my just debts and funeral expenses be paid out of my estate as
soon after my death as is practicable.

SECOND: I may leave a statement or list disposing of certain items of my tangible
personal property. Any such statement or list in existence at the time of my death shall be
determinative with respect to all items bequeathed therein.

THIRD: I give, devise, and bequeath all my estate, real, personal, and mixed, of whatever kind and wherever situated, of which I may die seized or possessed, or in which I may
have any interest or over which I may have any power of appointment or testamentary
disposition, to my children _____

_____

_____,

in equal shares, or their lineal descendants per capita.

FOURTH: In the event that any beneficiary fails to survive me by thirty days, then
this will shall take effect as if that person had predeceased me.

FIFTH: I hereby nominate, constitute, and appoint _____
as Personal Representative of this, my Last Will and Testament. In the event that such named
person is unable or unwilling to serve at any time or for any reason, then I nominate, constitute, and appoint _____ as Personal Representative in the
place and stead of the person first named herein. It is my will and I direct that my Personal
Representative shall not be required to furnish a bond for the faithful performance of his or
her duties in any jurisdiction, any provision of law to the contrary notwithstanding, and I give
my Personal Representative full power to administer my estate, including the power to settle claims, pay debts, and sell, lease or exchange real and personal property without court
order.

IN WITNESS WHEREOF, I declare this to be my Last Will and Testament and execute it willingly as my free and voluntary act for the purposes expressed herein and I am of
legal age and sound mind and make this under no constraint or undue influence, this _____
day of _____, _____ at _____ State of _____.

_____L.S.

The foregoing instrument was on said date subscribed at the end thereof by
_____ , the above named Testator who signed, pub-
lished, and declared this instrument to be his/her Last Will and Testament in the presence of
us and each of us, who thereupon at his/her request, in his/her presence, and in the presence
of each other, have hereunto subscribed our names as witnesses thereto. We are of sound
mind and proper age to witness a will and understand this to be his/her will, and to the best
of our knowledge testator is of legal age to make a will, of sound mind, and under no
constraint or undue influence.

_____residing at_____

_____residing at_____

Last Will and Testament

I, _____ a resident of _____ County, Pennsylvania do hereby make, publish, and declare this to be my Last Will and Testament, hereby revoking any and all Wills and Codicils heretofore made by me.

FIRST: I direct that all my just debts and funeral expenses be paid out of my estate as soon after my death as is practicable.

SECOND: I may leave a statement or list disposing of certain items of my tangible personal property. Any such statement or list in existence at the time of my death shall be determinative with respect to all items bequeathed therein.

THIRD: I give, devise, and bequeath all my estate, real, personal, and mixed, of whatever kind and wherever situated, of which I may die seized or possessed, or in which I may have any interest or over which I may have any power of appointment or testamentary disposition, to the following: _____
_____
_____,
or to the survivor of them.

FOURTH: In the event that any beneficiary fails to survive me by thirty days, then this will shall take effect as if that person had predeceased me.

FIFTH: I hereby nominate, constitute, and appoint _____ as Personal Representative of this, my Last Will and Testament. In the event that such named person is unable or unwilling to serve at any time or for any reason, then I nominate, constitute, and appoint _____ as Personal Representative in the place and stead of the person first named herein. It is my will and I direct that my Personal Representative shall not be required to furnish a bond for the faithful performance of his or her duties in any jurisdiction, any provision of law to the contrary notwithstanding, and I give my Personal Representative full power to administer my estate, including the power to settle claims, pay debts, and sell, lease or exchange real and personal property without court order.

IN WITNESS WHEREOF, I declare this to be my Last Will and Testament and execute it willingly as my free and voluntary act for the purposes expressed herein and I am of legal age and sound mind and make this under no constraint or undue influence, this _____ day of _____, _____ at _____ State of _____.

_____L.S.

The foregoing instrument was on said date subscribed at the end thereof by
_____, the above named Testator who signed, published, and declared this instrument to be his/her Last Will and Testament in the presence of us and each of us, who thereupon at his/her request, in his/her presence, and in the presence of each other, have hereunto subscribed our names as witnesses thereto. We are of sound mind and proper age to witness a will and understand this to be his/her will, and to the best of our knowledge testator is of legal age to make a will, of sound mind, and under no constraint or undue influence.

_____residing at_____

_____residing at_____

Last Will and Testament

I, _____ a resident of _____ County, Pennsylvania do hereby make, publish, and declare this to be my Last Will and Testament, hereby revoking any and all Wills and Codicils heretofore made by me.

FIRST: I direct that all my just debts and funeral expenses be paid out of my estate as soon after my death as is practicable.

SECOND: I may leave a statement or list disposing of certain items of my tangible personal property. Any such statement or list in existence at the time of my death shall be determinative with respect to all items bequeathed therein.

THIRD: I give, devise, and bequeath all my estate, real, personal, and mixed, of whatever kind and wherever situated, of which I may die seized or possessed, or in which I may have any interest or over which I may have any power of appointment or testamentary disposition, to the following _____

_____

_____,

in equal shares, or their lineal descendants per stirpes.

FOURTH: In the event that any beneficiary fails to survive me by thirty days, then this will shall take effect as if that person had predeceased me.

FIFTH: I hereby nominate, constitute, and appoint _____ as Personal Representative of this, my Last Will and Testament. In the event that such named person is unable or unwilling to serve at any time or for any reason, then I nominate, constitute, and appoint _____ as Personal Representative in the place and stead of the person first named herein. It is my will and I direct that my Personal Representative shall not be required to furnish a bond for the faithful performance of his or her duties in any jurisdiction, any provision of law to the contrary notwithstanding, and I give my Personal Representative full power to administer my estate, including the power to settle claims, pay debts, and sell, lease or exchange real and personal property without court order.

IN WITNESS WHEREOF, I declare this to be my Last Will and Testament and execute it willingly as my free and voluntary act for the purposes expressed herein and I am of legal age and sound mind and make this under no constraint or undue influence, this _____ day of _____, _____ at _____ State of _____.

_____L.S.

The foregoing instrument was on said date subscribed at the end thereof by
_____, the above named Testator who signed, pub-
lished, and declared this instrument to be his/her Last Will and Testament in the presence of
us and each of us, who thereupon at his/her request, in his/her presence, and in the presence
of each other, have hereunto subscribed our names as witnesses thereto. We are of sound
mind and proper age to witness a will and understand this to be his/her will, and to the best
of our knowledge testator is of legal age to make a will, of sound mind, and under no
constraint or undue influence.

_____residing at_____

_____residing at_____

Self-Proved Will Affidavit
(attach to Will)

COMMONWEALTH OF PENNSYLVANIA

COUNTY OF _____

    We, _____, _____,
and _____ the testator and the witnesses respectively,
whose names are signed to the attached or foregoing instrument, having been sworn,
declared to the undersigned officer that the testator, in the presence of witnesses, signed the
instrument as his/her last will, that he/she signed willingly and executed the will as his/her
free and voluntary act, that to the best of our knowledge the testator was at that time 18
years of age or older, of sound mind and under no constraint or undue influence, and that
each of the witnesses, in the presence of the testator and in the presence of each other, signed
the will as witnesses.

_____
Testator_____

_____
Witness_____

_____
Witness_____

    Subscribed and sworn to before me by _____ the testator, and by _____ and _____,
the witnesses, all of whom personally appeared before me on _____,
_____. The testator, _____ is personally known to me
or has produced_____ as identification,
_____ is personally known to me or has produced
_____ as identification _____
is personally known to me or has produced _____
as identification.

_____
Notary Public
My commission expires:
My commission number is:

(Notary Seal)

Codicil to the Will of

_____

I, _____, a resident of _____ County, Pennsylvania declare this to be the first codicil to my Last Will and Testament dated _____, _____.

FIRST: I hereby revoke the clause of my Will which reads as follows:
_____
_____
_____
_____.

SECOND: I hereby add the following clause to my Will: _____
_____
_____
_____.

THIRD: In all other respects I hereby confirm and republish my Last Will and Testament dated _____, _____.

IN WITNESS WHEREOF, I have signed, published, and declared the foregoing instrument as and for a codicil to my Last Will and Testament, this _____ day of _____, _____.

_____

The foregoing instrument was on the _____day of _____, _____, signed at the end thereof, and at the same time published and declared by _____, as and for a codicil to his/her Last Will and Testament, dated _____, _____, in the presence of each of us, who, this attestation clause having been read to us, did at the request of the said testator/testatrix, in his/her presence and in the presence of each other sign our names as witnesses thereto.

_____residing at_____

_____residing at_____

Self-Proved Codicil Affidavit
(attach to Codicil)

COMMONWEALTH OF PENNSYLVANIA

COUNTY OF _____

    We, _____, _____, and _____ the testator and the witnesses respectively, whose names are signed to the attached or foregoing instrument, having been sworn, declared to the undersigned officer that the testator, in the presence of witnesses, signed the instrument as his/her last will, that he/she signed willingly and executed the will as his/her free and voluntary act, that to the best of our knowledge the testator was at that time 18 years of age or older, of sound mind and under no constraint or undue influence, and that each of the witnesses, in the presence of the testator and in the presence of each other, signed the will as witnesses.

_____
Testator_____

_____
Witness_____

_____
Witness_____

    Subscribed and sworn to before me by _____ the testator, and by _____ and _____, the witnesses, all of whom personally appeared before me on _____, _____. The testator, _____ is personally known to me or has produced_____ as identification, _____ is personally known to me or has produced _____ as identification _____ is personally known to me or has produced _____ as identification.

_____
Notary Public
My commission expires:
My commission number is:

(Notary Seal)

Living Will

Declaration made this _____ day of _____, _____. I, _____, willfully and voluntarily make known my desire that my dying not be artificially prolonged under the circumstances set forth below, and I do hereby declare:

If at any time I have a terminal condition and if my attending or treating physician and another consulting physician have determined that there can be no medical probability of my recovery from such condition, I direct that life-prolonging procedures be withheld or withdrawn when the application of such procedures would serve only to prolong artificially the process of dying, and that I be permitted to die naturally with only the administration of medication or the performance of any medical procedure deemed necessary to provide me with comfort, care or alleviate pain.

It is my intention that this declaration be honored by my family and physician as the final expression of my legal right to refuse medical or surgical treatment and to accept the consequences for such refusal.

In the event that I have been determined to be unable to provide express and informed consent regarding the withholding, withdrawal, or continuation of life-prolonging procedures, I wish to designate, as my surrogate to carry out the provisions of this declaration:

Name:_____

Address:_____

_____ Zip Code:_____

Phone: _____

I understand the full import of this declaration, and am emotionally and mentally competent to make this declaration.

Additional instructions (optional):

_____

_____

_____

(Signed)

_____   _____

Witness   Witness

_____   _____

Address   Address

_____   _____

Phone   Phone

UNIFORM DONOR CARD

The undersigned hereby makes this anatomical gift, if medically acceptable, to take effect on death. The words and marks below indicate my desires:

I give:

      (a) ____ any needed organs or parts;

      (b) ____ only the following organs or parts

_____

for the purpose of transplantation, therapy, medical research, or education;

      (c) ____ my body for anatomical study if needed.

Limitations or special wishes, if any:

_____

Signed by the donor and the following witnesses in the presence of each other:

_____   _____
Signature of Donor   Date of birth

_____   _____
Date signed   City & State

_____   _____
Witness   Witness

_____   _____
Address   Address

UNIFORM DONOR CARD

The undersigned hereby makes this anatomical gift, if medically acceptable, to take effect on death. The words and marks below indicate my desires:

I give:

      (a) ____ any needed organs or parts;

      (b) ____ only the following organs or parts

_____

for the purpose of transplantation, therapy, medical research, or education;

      (c) ____ my body for anatomical study if needed.

Limitations or special wishes, if any:

_____

Signed by the donor and the following witnesses in the presence of each other:

_____   _____
Signature of Donor   Date of birth

_____   _____
Date signed   City & State

_____   _____
Witness   Witness

_____   _____
Address   Address

UNIFORM DONOR CARD

The undersigned hereby makes this anatomical gift, if medically acceptable, to take effect on death. The words and marks below indicate my desires:

I give:

      (a) ____ any needed organs or parts;

      (b) ____ only the following organs or parts

for the purpose of transplantation, therapy, medical research, or education;

      (c) ____ my body for anatomical study if needed.

Limitations or special wishes, if any:

_____

Signed by the donor and the following witnesses in the presence of each other:

_____   _____
Signature of Donor   Date of birth

_____   _____
Date signed   City & State

_____   _____
Witness   Witness

_____   _____
Address   Address

UNIFORM DONOR CARD

The undersigned hereby makes this anatomical gift, if medically acceptable, to take effect on death. The words and marks below indicate my desires:

I give:

      (a) ____ any needed organs or parts;

      (b) ____ only the following organs or parts

_____

for the purpose of transplantation, therapy, medical research, or education;

      (c) ____ my body for anatomical study if needed.

Limitations or special wishes, if any:

_____

Signed by the donor and the following witnesses in the presence of each other:

_____   _____
Signature of Donor   Date of birth

_____   _____
Date signed   City & State

_____   _____
Witness   Witness

_____   _____
Address   Address

One of these cards should be cut out and carried in your wallet or purse.

Glossary

administrator (*administratrix* if female). A person appointed by the court to oversee distribution of the property of someone who died (either without a will, or if the person designated in the will is unable to serve).

attested will. A will which includes an attestation clause and has been signed in front of witnesses.

beneficiary. A person who is entitled to receive property from a person who died (regardless of whether there is a will).

bequest. Personal property left to someone in a will.

children's trust. A trust set up to hold property given to children. Usually it provides that the children will not receive their property until they reach a higher age than the age of majority.

codicil. An amendment to a will.

community property. Property acquired by a husband and wife by their labors during their marriage.

decedent. A person who has died.

descendent. A child, grandchild, great-grandchild, etc.

devise. Real property left to someone in a will. A person who is entitled to a devise is called a *devisee*.

elective share. In non-community property states, the portion of the estate which may be taken by a surviving spouse, regardless of what the will says.

executor (*executrix* if female). A person appointed in a will to oversee distribution of the property of someone who died with a will. However, today this person is called a *personal representative*.

exempt property. Property that is exempt from distribution as a normal part of the estate.

family allowance. An amount of money set aside from the estate to support the family of the decedent for a period of time.

forced share. *See* **elective share**.

heir. A person who will inherit from a decedent who died without a will.

holographic will. A will in which all of the material provisions are entirely in the handwriting on the maker.

intestate. Without making a will. One who dies without a will is said to have *died intestate*.

intestate share. In non-community property states, the portion of the estate a spouse is entitled to receive if there is no will.

joint tenancy. A type of property ownership by two or more persons, in which if one owner dies, that owner's interest goes to the other joint tenants (not to the deceased owner's heirs as in tenancy in common).

legacy. Real property left to someone in a will. A person who is entitled to a legacy is called a *legatee*.

living will. A document expressing the writer's desires regarding how medical care is to be handled in the event the writer is not able to express his or her wishes concerning the use of life-prolonging medical procedures.

per capita. Distribution of property with equal shares going to each person.

per stirpes. Distribution of property with equal shares going to each family line.

personal representative. A person appointed by the court, or will, to oversee distribution of the property of the person who died. This is a more modern term than "administrator," "executor," etc., and applies regardless of whether there is a will.

probate. The process of settling a decedent's estate through the probate court.

residue. The property that is left over in an estate after all specific bequests and devises.

self-proving affidavit. A form added to a will in which the will maker and witnesses state under oath that they have signed and witnessed the will.

specific bequest *or* **specific devise**. A gift in a will of a specific item of property, or a specific amount of cash.

statutory will. A will which has been prepared according to the requirements of a statute.

tenancy by the entirety. A type of property ownership by a married couple, in which the property automatically passes to one spouse upon the death of the other. This is basically the same as joint tenancy, except that it is only between a husband and wife.

tenancy in common. Ownership of property by two or more people, in which each owner's share would descend to that owner's heirs (not to the other owners as in joint tenancy).

testate. With a will. One who dies with a will is said to have *died testate*.

testator. (*testatrix* if female.) A person who makes his or her will.

INDEX

Your #1 Source for Real World Legal Information...

SPHINX® PUBLISHING
A Division of Sourcebooks, Inc.®
- Written by lawyers
- Simple English explanation of the law
- Forms and instructions included

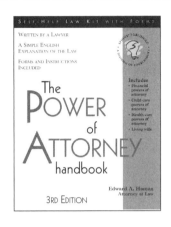

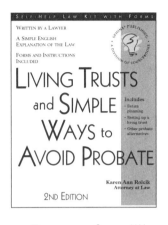

HOW TO FILE FOR DIVORCE IN PENNSYLVANIA

A simple guide for obtaining a divorce in Pennsylvania. This book provides essential information concerning property division, grounds for divorce, child custody issues and more. Includes forms to file with instructions.

152 pages; $19.95;
ISBN 1-57071-177-1

POWER OF ATTORNEY HANDBOOK, 3RD ED.

Provides information concerning power of attorney laws. It also explains when and why you need power of attorney. Includes forms to file and instructions.

218 pages; $19.95;
ISBN 1-57071-348-0

LIVING TRUSTS AND SIMPLE WAYS TO AVOID PROBATE, 2ND ED.

This book explains what probate is, the advantages and disadvantages of probate and more. Provides information on alternatives to probate, including: joint ownership, life insurance and land trusts. Includes necessary forms to file plus instructions.

166 pages; $19.95;
ISBN 1-57071-336-7

See the following order form for books written specifically for California, Florida, Georgia, Illinois, Massachusetts, Michigan, Minnesota, New York, North Carolina, Pennsylvania, and Texas! *Coming soon—Ohio and New Jersey!*

Sphinx Publishing's Legal Survival Guides
are directly available from the Sourcebooks, Inc., or from your local bookstores.
For credit card orders call 1–800–43–BRIGHT, write P.O. Box 372, Naperville, IL 60566,
or fax 630-961-2168

SPHINX® PUBLISHING'S NATIONAL TITLES

Valid in All 50 States

LEGAL SURVIVAL IN BUSINESS

How to Form a Limited Liability Company (April)	$19.95
How to Form Your Own Corporation (2E)	$19.95
How to Form Your Own Partnership	$19.95
How to Register Your Own Copyright (2E)	$19.95
How to Register Your Own Trademark (2E)	$19.95
Most Valuable Business Legal Forms You'll Ever Need (2E)	$19.95
Most Valuable Corporate Forms You'll Ever Need (2E)	$24.95
Software Law (with diskette)	$29.95

LEGAL SURVIVAL IN COURT

Crime Victim's Guide to Justice	$19.95
Debtors' Rights (3E)	$12.95
Defend Yourself against Criminal Charges	$19.95
Grandparents' Rights (2E)	$19.95
Help Your Lawyer Win Your Case	$12.95
Jurors' Rights (2E)	$9.95
Legal Malpractice and Other Claims against Your Lawyer (2E) (June)	$18.95
Legal Research Made Easy (2E)	$14.95
Simple Ways to Protect Yourself from Lawsuits	$24.95
Victims' Rights	$12.95
Winning Your Personal Injury Claim	$19.95

LEGAL SURVIVAL IN REAL ESTATE

How to Buy a Condominium or Townhome	$16.95
How to Negotiate Real Estate Contracts (3E)	$16.95
How to Negotiate Real Estate Leases (3E)	$16.95
Successful Real Estate Brokerage Management	$19.95

LEGAL SURVIVAL IN PERSONAL AFFAIRS

How to File Your Own Bankruptcy (4E)	$19.95
How to File Your Own Divorce (3E)	$19.95
How to Make Your Own Will	$12.95
How to Write Your Own Living Will	$9.95
How to Write Your Own Premarital Agreement (2E)	$19.95
How to Win Your Unemployment Compensation Claim	$19.95
Living Trusts and Simple Ways to Avoid Probate (2E)	$19.95
Neighbors' Rights	$12.95
The Power of Attorney Handbook (3E)	$19.95
Simple Ways to Protect Yourself from Lawsuits	$24.95
Social Security Benefits Handbook (2E)	$14.95
Unmarried Parents' Rights	$19.95
U.S.A. Immigration Guide (3E)	$19.95
Guia de Inmigracion a Estados Unidos (2E) (May)	$19.95

Legal Survival Guides are directly available from Sourcebooks, Inc., or from your local bookstores.

For credit card orders call 1–800–43–BRIGHT, write P.O. Box 372, Naperville, IL 60566, or fax 630-961-2168

SPHINX® PUBLISHING ORDER FORM

BILL TO:		SHIP TO:	
Phone #	Terms	F.O.B. Chicago, IL	Ship Date

Charge my: ☐ VISA   ☐ MasterCard   ☐ American Express

☐ **Money Order or Personal Check**

Credit Card Number

Expiration Date

Qty	ISBN	Title	Retail	Ext.
		SPHINX PUBLISHING NATIONAL TITLES		
___	1-57071-166-6	Crime Victim's Guide to Justice	$19.95	___
___	1-57071-342-1	Debtors' Rights (3E)	$12.95	___
___	1-57071-162-3	Defend Yourself against Criminal Charges	$19.95	___
___	1-57248-082-3	Grandparents' Rights (2E)	$19.95	___
___	1-57248-087-4	Guia de Inmigracion a Estados Unidos (2E) (May)	$19.95	___
___	1-57248-021-1	Help Your Lawyer Win Your Case	$12.95	___
___	1-57071-164-X	How to Buy a Condominium or Townhome	$16.95	___
___	1-57071-223-9	How to File Your Own Bankruptcy (4E)	$19.95	___
___	1-57071-224-7	How to File Your Own Divorce (3E)	$19.95	___
___	1-57248-083-1	How to Form a Limited Liability Company (April)	$19.95	___
___	1-57071-227-1	How to Form Your Own Corporation (2E)	$19.95	___
___	1-57071-343-X	How to Form Your Own Partnership	$19.95	___
___	1-57071-228-X	How to Make Your Own Will	$12.95	___
___	1-57071-331-6	How to Negotiate Real Estate Contracts (3E)	$16.95	___
___	1-57071-332-4	How to Negotiate Real Estate Leases (3E)	$16.95	___
___	1-57071-225-5	How to Register Your Own Copyright (2E)	$19.95	___
___	1-57071-226-3	How to Register Your Own Trademark (2E)	$19.95	___
___	1-57071-349-9	How to Win Your Unemployment Compensation Claim	$19.95	___
___	1-57071-167-4	How to Write Your Own Living Will	$9.95	___
___	1-57071-344-8	How to Write Your Own Premarital Agreement (2E)	$19.95	___
___	1-57071-333-2	Jurors' Rights (2E)	$9.95	___
___	1-57248-090-4	Legal Malpractice and Other Claims against...(2E) (June)	$18.95	___
___	1-57071-400-2	Legal Research Made Easy (2E)	$14.95	___
___	1-57071-336-7	Living Trusts and Simple Ways to Avoid Probate (2E)	$19.95	___
___	1-57071-345-6	Most Valuable Bus. Legal Forms You'll Ever Need (2E)	$19.95	___
___	1-57071-346-4	Most Valuable Corporate Forms You'll Ever Need (2E)	$24.95	___

Qty	ISBN	Title	Retail	Ext.
___	1-57248-089-0	Neighbors' Rights	$12.95	___
___	1-57071-348-0	The Power of Attorney Handbook (3E)	$19.95	___
___	1-57248-020-3	Simple Ways to Protect Yourself from Lawsuits	$24.95	___
___	1-57071-337-5	Social Security Benefits Handbook (2E)	$14.95	___
___	1-57071-163-1	Software Law (w/diskette)	$29.95	___
___	0-913825-86-7	Successful Real Estate Brokerage Mgmt.	$19.95	___
___	1-57071-399-5	Unmarried Parents' Rights	$19.95	___
___	1-57071-354-5	U.S.A. Immigration Guide (3E)	$19.95	___
___	0-913825-82-4	Victims' Rights	$12.95	___
___	1-57071-165-8	Winning Your Personal Injury Claim	$19.95	___
		CALIFORNIA TITLES		
___	1-57071-360-X	CA Power of Attorney Handbook	$12.95	___
___	1-57071-355-3	How to File for Divorce in CA	$19.95	___
___	1-57071-356-1	How to Make a CA Will	$12.95	___
___	1-57071-408-8	How to Probate an Estate in CA (April)	$19.95	___
___	1-57071-357-X	How to Start a Business in CA	$16.95	___
___	1-57071-358-8	How to Win in Small Claims Court in CA	$14.95	___
___	1-57071-359-6	Landlords' Rights and Duties in CA	$19.95	___
		FLORIDA TITLES		
___	1-57071-363-4	Florida Power of Attorney Handbook (2E)	$12.95	___
___	1-57248-093-9	How to File for Divorce in FL (6E) (July)	$21.95	___
___	1-57248-086-6	How to Form a Limited Liability Co. in FL (April)	$19.95	___
___	1-57071–401-0	How to Form a Partnership in FL	$19.95	___
___	1-57071-380-4	How to Form a Corporation in FL (4E)	$19.95	___
___	1-57071-361-8	How to Make a FL Will (5E)	$12.95	___
___	1-57248-088-2	How to Modify Your FL Divorce Judgement (4E)(May)	$22.95	___
___		***Form Continued on Following Page***	**SUBTOTAL**	

To order, call Sourcebooks at 1-800-43-BRIGHT or FAX (630)961-2168 (Bookstores, libraries, wholesalers—please call for discount)

SPHINX® PUBLISHING ORDER FORM

Qty	ISBN	Title	Retail	Ext.
		FLORIDA TITLES (CONT'D)		
____	1-57071-364-2	How to Probate an Estate in FL (3E)	$24.95	____
____	1-57248-081-5	How to Start a Business in FL (5E) (March)	$16.95	____
____	1-57071-362-6	How to Win in Small Claims Court in FL (6E)	$14.95	____
____	1-57071-335-9	Landlords' Rights and Duties in FL (7E)	$19.95	____
____	1-57071-334-0	Land Trusts in FL (5E)	$24.95	____
____	0-913825-73-5	Women's Legal Rights in FL	$19.95	____
		GEORGIA TITLES		
____	1-57071-376-6	How to File for Divorce in GA (3E)	$19.95	____
____	1-57248-075-0	How to Make a GA Will (3E)	$12.95	____
____	1-57248-076-9	How to Start a Business in Georgia (3E)	$16.95	____
		ILLINOIS TITLES		
____	1-57071-405-3	How to File for Divorce in IL (2E)	$19.95	____
____	1-57071-415-0	How to Make an IL Will (2E)	$12.95	____
____	1-57071-416-9	How to Start a Business in IL (2E)	$16.95	____
____	1-57248-078-5	Landlords' Rights & Duties in IL (February)	$19.95	____
		MASSACHUSETTS TITLES		
____	1-57071-329-4	How to File for Divorce in MA (2E)	$19.95	____
____	1-57248-050-5	How to Make a MA Will	$9.95	____
____	1-57248-053-X	How to Probate an Estate in MA	$19.95	____
____	1-57248-054-8	How to Start a Business in MA	$16.95	____
____	1-57248-055-6	Landlords' Rights and Duties in MA	$19.95	____
		MICHIGAN TITLES		
____	1-57071-409-6	How to File for Divorce in MI (2E)	$19.95	____
____	1-57248-077-7	How to Make a MI Will (2E)	$12.95	____
____	1-57071-407-X	How to Start a Business in MI (2E)	$16.95	____
		MINNESOTA TITLES		
____	1-57248-039-4	How to File for Divorce in MN	$19.95	____
____	1-57248-040-8	How to Form a Simple Corporation in MN	$19.95	____
____	1-57248-037-8	How to Make a MN Will	$9.95	____
____	1-57248-038-6	How to Start a Business in MN	$16.95	____
		NEW YORK TITLES		

Qty	ISBN	Title	Retail	Ext.
____	1-57071-184-4	How to File for Divorce in NY (March)	$19.95	____
____	1-57248-095-5	How to Make a NY Will (2E)	$12.95	____
____	1-57071-185-2	How to Start a Business in NY	$16.95	____
____	1-57071-187-9	How to Win in Small Claims Court in NY	$14.95	____
____	1-57071-186-0	Landlords' Rights and Duties in NY (March)	$19.95	____
____	1-57071-188-7	New York Power of Attorney Handbook	$19.95	____
		NORTH CAROLINA TITLES		
____	1-57071-326-X	How to File for Divorce in NC (2E)	$19.95	____
____	1-57071-327-8	How to Make a NC Will (2E)	$12.95	____
____	1-57248-096-3	How to Start a Business in NC (2E)	$16.95	____
____	1-57248-091-2	Landlords' Rights & Duties in NC (June)	$19.95	____
		PENNSYLVANIA TITLES		
____	1-57071-177-1	How to File for Divorce in PA	$19.95	____
____	1-57248-094-7	How to Make a PA Will (2E)	$12.95	____
____	1-57071-178-X	How to Start a Business in PA	$16.95	____
____	1-57071-179-8	Landlords' Rights and Duties in PA (June)	$19.95	____
		TEXAS TITLES		
____	1-57071-330-8	How to File for Divorce in TX (2E)	$19.95	____
____	1-57248-009-2	How to Form a Simple Corporation in TX	$19.95	____
____	1-57071-417-7	How to Make a TX Will (2E)	$12.95	____
____	1-57071-418-5	How to Probate an Estate in TX (2E)	$19.95	____
____	1-57071-365-0	How to Start a Business in TX (2E)	$16.95	____
____	1-57248-012-2	How to Win in Small Claims Court in TX	$14.95	____
____	1-57248-011-4	Landlords' Rights and Duties in TX	$19.95	____

SUBTOTAL THIS PAGE ____

SUBTOTAL PREVIOUS PAGE ____

Illinois residents add 6.75% sales tax
Florida residents add 6% state sales tax plus applicable discretionary surtax

Shipping— $4.00 for 1st book, $1.00 each additional ____

TOTAL ____